"God uses many unique items from the Scriptures and from what He has created to communicate and guide us in life. He directs our path and cares for us during difficult times. *A Second Chance from Heaven* has many helpful applications for anyone dealing with life's challenges. Definitely a must read."

Dr. Gene Mayhew
Professor of Old Testament
Moody Theological Seminary

"*A Second Chance from Heaven* is an inspiring testimony of faith and redemption in a broken world. As a minister and author with autism, I could relate personally with David's social struggles, desire for acceptance, and feelings of rejection. Todd beautifully illustrates through the Scriptures and his son's spiritual journey the power of Christ to transform all things, even Asperger's, into His glory. David's life provides hope and encouragement to every person experiencing doubt and questioning God's love and purpose."

Ron Sandison, founder of Spectrum Inclusion, author of *A Parent's Guide to Autism: Practical Advice. Biblical Wisdom.*

"*A Second Chance from Heaven* is a wonderfully crafted story of the love of a father and the dependency on God through tough times. It is an awe-inspiring reminder of the miracle of life. The story of David and Todd is a story of hope, family, and of second chances from God."

Greg McDougall, Director of Special Needs Ministry
Woodside Bible Church

A Second Chance from Heaven

A Near Death Experience
Restores Purpose for a Father and Son

Todd A. Gillert

May the Lord Bless you

Todd Gillert

10/17/16

Gazelle PRESS

Mobile, Alabama

A Second Chance from Heaven
by Todd A. Gillert
Copyright ©2016 Todd A. Gillert

Unless otherwise identified, Scripture is taken from *THE HOLY BIBLE: New International Version* ©1978 by the New York International Bible Society, used by permission of Zondervan Bible Publishers.

ISBN 978-1-58169-642-4
For Worldwide Distribution
Printed in the U.S.A.
Gazelle Press
P.O. Box 191540 • Mobile, AL 36619
800-367-8203

Table of Contents

Acknowledgments

I wish to acknowledge the very talented medical teams of the University of Michigan Medical Center in Ann Arbor, William Beaumont Health Care System of Troy, the Survival Flight crew, and the Rehabilitation Unit of Crittenton Hospital in Rochester, Michigan, for the life-saving healthcare provided to David. They were amazing in their efforts to treat his extremely rare illness. The University of Michigan's Burn Trauma Unit was outstanding in their dedication to anticipate David's symptoms as the disease progressed as well as compassionately provided timely information on his condition as we searched for hope in every update.

I am extremely grateful to Dr. Christopher Remishofsky M.D. of Georgetown Dermatologists who initially recognized David's condition as Stevens-Johnson-Syndrome (SJS TEN). His superior diagnostic skills and quick response in making the Survival Flight arrangements dramatically improved David's outcome.

I would like to thank Portraits Plus of Davison, Michigan, for providing several portraits used throughout the book. I would also like to acknowledge Promiseland Inspirations for providing the photos of the Holy Land as well as Katharine O"Keefe for her contribution to David's story through her painting of "The Lamb."

I would like to express my deep appreciation to my extended family, friends, church family, pastors, and prayer warriors whose encouragement and prayers have brought us through these trying times. I am so grateful to have this incredible support group stand with us during the darkest hours.

A very special thanks and love to my wife and sons. They are my constant source of joy and happiness and without them this book would not have been possible.

Finally, and most importantly, I would like to thank God for His leading, guiding, healing and abiding presence in my life as well as that of my family. I am abundantly grateful He intervenes in the lives of ordinary people as He shows His love for mankind.

Introduction

Have you ever wished you could begin again and erase an event in your life that caused you great pain? Have you ever wondered if God could ever help you pick up the shattered pieces of your life? On the tenth anniversary of my oldest son's death, I witnessed my second son, David, endure a rare disease that caused his skin to peel away from his body as he barely clung to life. In the darkest agony any soul can endure, I helplessly watched and waited for a miracle. For weeks, my faith would be tested time and time again. By every measurement, these events tell a story of doom and gloom, a story of complete failure and desperation as I wondered if death would claim another of my sons.

Out of the deepest pit of pain, God provided a second chance from heaven. He used these very unexpected circumstances to physically and emotionally heal my son and redeem the harshest sorrow of my life.

While David lay motionless in the ICU, the beauty of heaven touched him as angels guided the way to the security of paradise. A majestic tree of magnificent light adorned the sacred ground. The light and peace of God radiated the grandeur of perfection and serenity in that place.

David's experience has filled him with passion and purpose. His transformation has enabled him to share his story with people who need encouragement when dealing with difficult situations. He has a glorious message to share with people who fear the unknown dimensions of death. Heaven is real and the Lamb heals us from every affliction.

A Second Chance From Heaven is a story of hope that finds meaning in the midst of despair. It will capture your imagination as miracles unfold when God offers redemption through His power and love. Join me on this harrowing journey, and experience for yourself the wonders of God as He answers the prayers of ordinary people in a most unusual way.

~ 1 ~

Chaos into the Night

If I say, "Surely the darkness will hide me and the light become night around me," even the darkness will not be dark to you; the night will shine like the day, for darkness is as light to you (Psalm 139: 11-12).

On a cold February night in 2009, I blankly gazed at the stars outside the hospital room window. With tears in my eyes, I contemplated the magnitude of the devastation tomorrow could bring to my family. My oldest son, David, lay lethargic in the bed behind me. At the young age of twenty, he was dying from a rare illness. My feelings of helplessness and hopelessness paralyzed my spirit. I searched the deep recesses of my soul, wondering if God could hear my cry as I looked to the heavens for a miracle.

I was told that David had only hours to live if he did not get advanced care from a burn trauma unit located sixty miles away. When the doctor delivered the distressing news, I felt as if I were encompassed in an abyss of total despair. The moment was surreal as I reflected on how complicated his life had become.

Born with Asperger's syndrome, he had suffered for years with the challenges autism had placed upon him. He struggled in school and throughout his childhood. His experiences

1

in life were largely negative. He was not able to make friends, and it broke my heart.

I always dreamed that one day David's life would be filled with joy and laughter. I wanted him to have experiences similar to mine: an idyllic childhood with an abundance of friends. David, on the other hand, struggled to find just one friend and grew up in what would become a broken home. On this terrible night, all the pain, disappointments, and regrets that had haunted him throughout life seemed to fade into the background as death stalked him closely.

I was powerless to protect him as I was forced to endure this macabre scene. As his father, I had to be strong, but under this façade of strength, I cried for my son. His mother and I watched in disbelief as raw emotions tormented us. The significance of this dark night did not go unnoticed; it was the eve of another horrible nightmare. Exactly ten years earlier, our fifteen-year-old, first-born son, Michael, died suddenly.

This cruel twist of fate took my breath, leaving me numb. I could see my reflection in the window as I searched the heavens for a sign, just a glimmer of hope in this desperate situation. Emotionally, I was in a dismal fog, unable to cope and without strength. Physically, my energy was depleted and my movements were more like instinct. I knew I could not run, nor could I hide from the reality that was crushing my spirit.

The doctors worked frantically to coordinate the helicopter transfer from the local hospital to an advanced burn trauma unit that seemed so far away. I anxiously looked out the window to the western sky, yearning to see the beacon of light from a helicopter. I felt as if an hourglass was marking the passage of time, and only a few scarce moments remained. For an instant, each star in the cosmos became a ray of hope in my search. As I fixed my eyes on a distant starlight, hope faded as its shimmering light remained fixed in the heavens. Suddenly, in the distance, a small light shone above the horizon. This light moved slowly at first then gradually increased in size as it crossed the night sky and headed toward us. I could finally see the undeniable outline of a helicopter nearing the hospital. It began to hover at the emergency entrance and staked its claim on the earth below. The scene at the landing site was calm until the noise like that of a thousand winds descended from above. The thundering wind was violent as the parking lot debris scattered away from the landing site, forming a circle of uncontaminated space for the skids to touch. With precision landing, the Survival Flight set down at the emergency parking lot makeshift helipad as the crew rushed to retrieve my son.

Once David was safely aboard, the rotors began to labor once again with great power to raise his chariot into the heavens. I helplessly watched as the helicopter carried my precious child into the chaos of the night. The ferocious wind caused by the turbine engines subsided as the light from the beacon once again joined the chorus of the stars. Time seemed to stand still as David disappeared into the night sky, and in that horrific moment, I wondered if I would ever see my son alive again.

~ 2 ~

My Earthly Eden

*"For I know the plans I have for you," declares the Lord,
"plans to prosper you and not to harm you, plans to give
you hope and a future"* (Jeremiah 29:11).

I was born into a loving family in Lansing, Michigan. My
parents, Arnold and Morrine, lived with their growing family
in a small house on the outskirts of town. When I was a tod-
dler, my father was transferred from his job in Lansing to a
facility about eighty miles away in Pontiac. My parents
moved to nearby West Bloomfield Township, where they
purchased a home in an exceptional subdivision called
Westacres.

Our new two-story home had a small attached garage
and was located in the center of the subdivision on a beautiful
corner lot adjacent to a baseball field with two diamonds. My
first day in our new home did not go well at all. Evidently, I
was a curious child with an affinity for stair climbing. Much
to my mother's horror, I climbed to the top of the staircase
and toppled down, injuring my right leg. Fortunately, my first
experience did not set the tone for my childhood. My days in
Westacres only improved.

Looking back on my childhood, I realize I was fortunate
to have a great family and many friends. My brother Arnie

was the oldest of the five children, followed by my sisters June and Joan. I was the fourth child, and my sister Jeanne was born on my second birthday. Westacres was a unique, family-oriented community with many children and neighbor-friendly activities.

One weekend each summer, the entire subdivision gathered to compete in Field Day and Aquacade events. The festivities began with a Saturday morning parade, led by the Westacres fire truck. In a scene reminiscent of the Pied Piper, children joined the procession on bicycles adorned with ribbons and streamers. The parade followed behind the fire truck until it reached the baseball field by our home.

On the field children of all ages competed in games, including relays, three-legged races, baseball- and water balloon-throwing competitions, a pie-eating contest, and an egg toss. The following afternoon, the community gathered at the beach for the Aquacade, which included swimming and diving competitions.

The Westacres beach was on a small peninsula with shallow water on the west and deeper water on the east. Each summer, the young Westacres swimmers were divided into two groups: those who could swim well and those who could not. To earn the privilege of swimming on the deep side, each child had to complete a test and attain their Redcap. The Redcap was earned after a swimmer could cross from the shallow side to a floating dock, located approximately 120 feet away on the deep side of the beach. The entire swim was closely monitored by a lifeguard following in a nearby boat.

The Aquacade featured a variety of speed competitions. A pistol shot started the sixty-foot race, which ended at the shore. Competitors used five defined lanes in their quest for the gold. Additionally, high diving competitions took place from heights of five, seven, and eleven feet. Only the bravest souls took the exhilarating leap from the high dive.

Awards and ribbons were given to the top three competitors in each event. Each hard-earned ribbon was a source of great pride as the honorees stepped forward to claim their prize and the crowd of proud parents applauded.

Food vendors sold hot dogs, hamburgers, popcorn, cotton candy, ice cream, sodas, and snow cones. A dairy truck, complete with milk and ice cream, provided a perfect picnic atmosphere. In all my years of participation in these events, I cannot recall any rain interrupting either of the days, which defined the Westacres experience.

My childhood was full of fun and friendships. At the time, I did not fully appreciate what our community offered. In my innocence, I thought every community functioned this way. I remember asking my elementary school friends about their field day and aquacade activities. I was surprised to learn they did not have these types of community events. However, they were all aware of Westacres activities.

Westacres was well known locally, and years later, I learned the subdivision was on a national list of best places to live in the United States. It was the utopia many people can only dream about. The first time I watched the movie Pleasantville, I looked for the actor playing my role, as the show clearly depicted my childhood.

Recently, my wife and I struck up a conversation with some young adults who sat next to us in a restaurant. The young woman was wearing a varsity jacket from my alma mater, Walled Lake Central. In an attempt to start a friendly conversation, I mentioned I had grown up in Westacres. I could detect envy as they talked about the exclusivity and closeness of the community. We all laughed heartily when they called Westacres a community cult. Our new friends suggested outsiders are viewed as having a deprived childhood in comparison to the Westacres experience. The laughter increased dramatically when I said their suspicions were correct. The entire restaurant must have wondered why we were laughing so hard while I told stories from my childhood. Westacres is still an incredible community forty years later.

My childhood there is where my spiritual journey began. When I was a youngster, trying to understand the world, I looked into the night sky and wondered if God could see me. The sky was so large, and I was so small. Since the world was full of people and animals, I thought God might be too busy to notice me. Did He know I was thinking about Him? Did He care about me? These innocent questions of a child reached out to God, and I knew He was listening. My life was like a grain of sand on the seashore, yet God had somehow noticed me. Psalm 144:3 says, "Lord, what are human beings that you care for them, mere mortals that you think of them?"

In my early years, I sensed that God was near me. Although I could not see Him, it was as if He were in the next room. He was the unseen friend, guide, helper, and parent. His presence was subtle and somewhat near. I think children have the ability to see God in unique ways. Perhaps this is why Jesus speaks of angels abiding with them: "See that you do not despise one of these little ones. For I tell you that their angels in heaven always see the face of my Father in heaven" (Matthew 18:10).

I attended St. Marks Lutheran church with my family and was active there at an early age. I participated in church activities and served as an altar boy. I remember enjoying lighting the candles at the altar. I memorized the commandments and the articles of faith. I had a passion for learning about God and listened to the pastor proclaim that we must believe the Gospel. He repeated this phrase on a weekly basis, but I did not understand what he meant by the statement. I listened intently and pondered the sermons as I began to learn about the Scriptures and faith. This was the beginning of my spiritual formation. The tapestry of my life took shape as my concept of God developed.

One warm summer day when I was nine, I felt the presence and calling of God. I was outside in my backyard, standing in the sun and experiencing the beauty of the day. Intense light surrounded me. It was as if I were standing in a football stadium in bright daylight with the stadium lights shining directly on me. The light had a penetrating presence. The normal feelings of heat, cold, and wind did not exist in that moment. The beauty of the penetrating light was an awesome encounter. I recall the bright sun and blue sky, but my surroundings were somehow muted or unimportant. It was as if time had somehow stopped. My mind filled with ideas that did not originate from me, but I did not know how to process these thoughts. I believed God was near and felt as though He was in the light.

I believe God was making Himself known to me, although I did not tell my family or anyone else about the experience. Afterwards, I thought about this event and sought to better understand God. I interpreted this experience of light as a small and subtle introduction to the presence of

God. The childlike faith of my youth has stayed with me to this day. I tend to confound people by the simplicity of my faith because I view coincidences as actual acts of God. Today, I often feel purposely connected to Him. The bright-light experience eclipsed all subsequent events and was truly an amazing encounter.

I have heard many adults dwell upon painful memories and experiences they suffered in childhood. They tend to focus on the negative events in their life and forget to remember the joy and love in growing up. Perhaps they have subconsciously suppressed the good memories in favor of the bad ones. I cannot imagine the pain they must have felt if they did not experience the love and support every child needs. Westacres was clearly different because each neighbor was like a parent. Whenever I did something wrong or got into trouble, my parents were the first to know.

In my teenage years, I continued to learn about faith and why it is important to believe in God. I had all the information and knowledge necessary to step out in faith. However, I lacked the proper motivation. I had a great family and many friends. I was a happy-go-lucky kid who did not get into much trouble. I instinctively knew I was a sinner, and that troubled me. But I lacked the urgency needed to bring about a repentant heart and mind.

~ 3 ~

The Crooked Path

Where can I go from your Spirit? Where can I flee from your presence? If I go up to the heavens, you are there; if I make my bed in the depths, you are there. If I rise on the wings of the dawn, if I settle on the far side of the sea, even there your hand will guide me, your right hand will hold me fast (Psalm 139:7-10).

After graduating from high school, I lived at home and attended college at a local university. I starting working for General Motors and bought my first new car. It was a blue-green metallic Chevrolet Monte Carlo with a V8 engine and a landau top and cost $4,200. As a result of my new financial independence, I thought I was breaking into adulthood. The world seemed full of possibilities, and I could pursue almost any dream I desired.

In the fall of 1976, I was nineteen years old and totally unprepared for the unfortunate circumstance that was about to invade my life. My mother, the heart and soul of our family, was diagnosed with cancer. The prognosis was grim. I remember crying and asking God to intercede. I did not want my mother to die, and in my desperation, I tried to bargain with God.

I promised to make some profound religious changes in

my life in an effort to appease God. But I did not get the feeling He was falling for my half-hearted offering. Perhaps He knew I would not follow through with my part of the bargain if the circumstances changed according to my request. The tapestry of God had brought me to this moment for a purpose. I finally set first things first and asked the Lord to forgive me for past transgressions and cultivate in me a new heart and mind according to His will. I still remember the physical manifestations of the event. I could feel the comforting hand of the Lord as I was born into His kingdom that night.

Each day, I put one foot ahead of the other as I was led to destinations unknown. Strange things started happening. People from church started telling me how God was going to use me in some way, a confirmation not confined to church members. People at work, friends, and family—all saw a distinct difference in me. I felt a calling within my spirit to serve God. However, I did not understand where my life's mosaic fit into God's tapestry.

One Sunday morning in 1979, during a church service, a young woman and little girl sat in front of me. The woman had long, dark hair, which was an intense distraction for me as the sunlight from the windows shone on it. When the service was over, I introduced myself and mentioned how well her little girl had behaved during the service. She told me her name was Anna, and she was babysitting this little girl for her friend. We talked briefly about the sermon and struck up a conversation about a new singles group forming the following week at the church. Anna told me she planned to attend the get-together and hoped to see me there.

When the group met, we shared our goals and dreams. I

often talked about my intent to follow a ministry career path. This dream was in my heart and had followed me from the age of nine. I did not want a life of potential church service to be a surprise to Anna. Our relationship grew stronger and the following summer we were married. Within two years, I was attending a Lutheran college in Ann Arbor, where my dream of ministry was beginning to take shape.

My life was on track and I felt as if a career in ministry was just around the corner. I loved learning about the Bible and studying theology. But as my studies progressed, I encountered significant philosophical differences with what I was being taught that I could not ignore. Eventually, I had a falling out with one of my teachers. I thought it wise to withdraw from the school to reflect on my faith. The notion of pastoral ministry took on new dimensions in my life, and I looked for a way to balance what seemed to be conflicting goals as my life moved forward.

When I left college, my mother was nearing the end of her battle with cancer. She had fought this tenacious disease with all her strength. She had survived several operations and several rounds of chemotherapy. She refused to complain about her circumstances even though she was losing the battle. Her strength and resolve to fight her cancer was amazing to witness. It was difficult for me to watch her struggle and suffer. Throughout her entire ordeal, she displayed the grace and hope of finding peace with God. I watched the hand of God work in the entire family as we dealt with the reality of her sickness. Understanding the brevity of her mortality, she never lost sight of the blessings of life.

Ultimately, everyone rallied and worked together to bring

joy and happiness to her in her last years. On the day prior to her death, she lay in a comatose state on a bed in her home. I knew the end was near. I spoke these words to her from John 14:1-3, even though I had no indication she could hear me. Jesus said, "Do not let your hearts be troubled. You believe in God; believe also in me. My Father's house has many rooms; if that were not so, would I have told you that I am going there to prepare a place for you? And if I go and prepare a place for you, I will come back and take you to be with me that you also may be where I am."

She had no response and I knew the end was near. We called an ambulance to take her to the hospital because we did not know what else to do. She never regained consciousness.

Our family was at her bedside at the hospital when she died. Earlier in the day, I had taken my aunt and uncle home and then rushed back to the hospital. My assembled family did not think I would make it to see her one last time, but my brother Arnie told everyone she would hold on to life as she waited for me to arrive.

I reached her room just minutes before she died. The room was quiet and the mood was somber as we watched her fade away. She was not conscious as she struggled for breath. One breath followed another; however, the duration between breaths grew greater. Five seconds passed, followed by ten, then twenty, and thirty. We waited for one more breath, but it never came. Her life was over. I said a prayer for our family in the wake of our sorrow.

My wife, father, and I left the hospital to the sounds of pouring rain. I have always loved severe weather and have had a fascination with rain. Often I sit on the porch, captivated by the sound as it plummets to earth. For most of us, rain is not considered a blessing, and so we stay inside to avoid it. We will do most anything to keep from getting wet, and we complain about the weather. A rainy day is just another way of saying, "I'm having a bad day," and I was having an extremely bad day.

In the gospel of Matthew, rain is given to the just and unjust alike: ""That you may be children of your Father in heaven. He causes his sun to rise on the evil and the good, and sends rain on the righteous and the unrighteous" (Matthew 5:45). I used to think this passage meant that God sends blessings (sun) just as He sends curses (rain). To me, these torrents of rain were reminiscent of tears. But my father expressed a different view of the pouring rain. He believed rain was a sign from God that everything would be okay for our family. Evidently, he could see a rainbow in his mind's eye; whereas I could see only rain. Perhaps my father was right when he viewed rain as a blessing.

The valley of weeping caused by my mother's death would not ultimately define our family. We remembered her strength and courage as we laid her to rest. At her gravesite, I served as the minister for her memorial service, and a large number of people from the local community attended. This was my first experience in ministry. I read the traditional scriptures and talked about my memories of her. My brother also spoke of her love of family, friends, and the local community and gave a touching message of peace and tranquility. Although my mother was gone, her memory and love of family still lived in my heart.

Three years into my marriage, my first son, Michael, was born. Our family grew larger five years later with the addition of David, and became complete three years later with Stephen. Initially, our marriage was much like other marriages. There were great moments and there were moments of reflection. Being an optimist, I focused on the great moments. I now know the moments of reflection were more important to the marriage than the great moments. Nevertheless, I loved my family. I loved my wife and I loved my life. Life was good for a time.

As my responsibilities pressed in on me, my dream of entering the ministry faded fast. I did not see any way I could answer the call on my life. I was too busy making a living to change vocations. My heart was in ministry; however, my mind obviously was not. I always believed the timing wasn't right to follow my dream. When you think about the Old Testament patriarchs, you realize that a great deal of time usually lapsed between the call of God and its fulfillment. For example, God told Abraham that he and Sarah would have a son, and twenty-four years later, the promised son was born. Ecclesiastes 3:1 tells us there is a time for everything and a season for every activity under the heavens. Timing is everything, especially God's timing. Watching and waiting was difficult for me.

Our goals and dreams as a couple were changing radically. The foundational vision shifted and my dreams faded. In the 1990s, my calling to ministry had all but turned to dust. My marriage was falling apart, and there seemed to be little I could do about it. My wife and I were going through issues that seemed minuscule compared to the problems of other couples. I believed we could work through them and put them behind us. I was wrong.

The issues of discord grew. We couldn't reach a compromise on our disagreement. Sadly, conflict was all that remained in our hearts. We continued together for several years before the idea of divorce became a reality. In the fall of 1998, our marriage was over.

~ 4 ~

When Death Knocks

The Lord is close to the brokenhearted and saves those who are crushed in spirit (Psalm 34:18).

My oldest son, Michael, was sensitive, fun-loving, and brilliant. He excelled in school and had wonderful friends. He was soft spoken and his laughter was contagious. The retail computer industry was in its infancy when I bought him his first computer. In the 1990s, he was a computer geek using an IBM desktop and loved to write his own programs. His first program was entitled "Family Information." This program functioned like a spreadsheet, categorizing the important details of families. He looked for ways to market his program to computer users on the Internet. He experimented with a variety of potential trendy names for his new endeavor before settling on Gtechsoft. His computer skills became so advanced, I saw him as a tech prodigy.

He had blond hair and blue eyes and a tall, slender build. At 6'1", he was taller than most of his classmates. He had a heart that was gentle and kind to others and never gave us one day of grief throughout his entire life. He was the type of son many parents pray for, and I felt honored to be his father.

In early February 1999, I moved back to our family home as Anna and I tried to rebuild our relationship and restore our family. Later that month, our family suffered a horrible tragedy. I was at work at General Motors when my boss told me I was needed immediately at home. I could see fear and discomfort in his eyes as he avoided discussing any particulars. I had a sick feeling in my stomach, knowing something was terribly wrong. Security personnel drove me home, and I was frightened because I knew disaster awaited me.

I began to think through the various scenarios. It was early in the afternoon before school let out, so my children should be safe. I concluded the problem must be with Anna. As I approached the driveway, there were cars everywhere, including police cars and a coroner's car. I now understood the severity of the situation. In a state of panic and shock, I walked up the driveway and across the front lawn through newly fallen snow. I had no idea what the next few minutes would bring.

Inside, people milled around everywhere. Our pastor's wife and the associate pastor met me at the door but said nothing. I still believed the problem was with Anna, until a policeman said that my wife had something to tell me. Those words pierced my soul because I now knew that the coroner's car was there for a child. I remember thinking about my three children and wondering which one was dead. Terror filled my mind as I tried to wrestle with the horrific news. A second thought, infinitely more nightmarish, surfaced. How many?

No words can adequately describe my feelings as I waited to hear the news. For just one moment, in my mind, each of my children was still alive—a moment that quickly faded away.

Anna delivered the news that our oldest son Michael was dead. I do not know if shock or anger could fully describe my feelings. All the joy and blessing Michael brought to our family— gone in an instant. His presence and smile were gone forever. My fifteen-year-old son was dead in the basement directly beneath me, and there was nothing anyone could do. It was the worst day of my life. Nothing in this world can pierce your soul as quickly or cut more deeply than losing a child.

Anna and I somehow had to explain Michael's death to our younger sons, but how? We were living in the midst of a nightmare. Anna proceeded to tell our sons what had happened to Michael. Both boys cried and we cried as a family as we tried to comfort one another in our sorrow.

Over the next few days, I replayed events in my life as snapshots and tried to attach meaning to what had happened to Michael. My relationship with Anna was stressed beyond belief. Both of us looked for answers where none could be found. Somewhere in the ruins of our thoughts, we shared a common pain and common regret. Like other couples, we had a history of petty arguments that had seemed important at the time.

I often wonder if we missed a cry for help from our son. Down deep in my heart, I refused to acknowledge Michael's part in his own death. Rather, I blamed his mother and myself for destroying a beautiful family. I was angry at what had happened. I was extremely disappointed in both of us, and it was hard not to lash out against her. I started working through my own feelings, and I knew blaming her was not the answer, nor was this her fault. Michael, for reasons unknown, had made a horrible decision.

I felt as if my heart had a giant hole that could never be filled. As a result, sorrow and grief filled my life. I was in such despair that I could no longer laugh at anything nor escape into a world of joy. It was as if my laughter nerve had died. I could not find purpose or meaning in any of life's events. Everything was shrouded in a cloud of fog. The colors of trees and grass as well as all creation seemed dull, as I could no longer enjoy anything. My faith was crushed as the worst pain a parent could experience became my existence.

Darkness was everywhere as I followed the routine of life, looking for consolation. In time, I stumbled across Psalm 139:16: "Your eyes saw my unformed body; all the days ordained for me were written in your book before one of them came to be." This passage finally brought peace to my mind when I understood God had numbered Michael's days before he was born. Somehow, understanding God's ways removed the torment of a life cut short. I cannot imagine how much debris God had to place in my path before I looked up to Him for answers.

As the days turned to weeks and then to months, my life slowly began again. Laughter awakened within me. I began to see the beauty of color in creation once again. With each passing day, my color pallet was slightly stimulated as I noticed the subtleties of nature. Anna and I again tried to rebuild our relationship and restore a foundation that had been largely destroyed.

Our house had become an emotional liability because it was there our son died. I was tormented on a daily basis, thinking about the events that happened in the basement. I hated descending that stairway. I felt as if I were underwater and unable to breathe. I moved about the area in a panic, finishing my tasks, and returning from what I considered Hades. We moved from the family home in a desperate attempt to escape the shadow of death covering the dwelling. Anna and I were given a second chance for a relationship. A year and half later, we decided to remarry, thereby bringing the broken pieces of our family back together.

~ 5 ~

David's Early Years

So do not fear, for I am with you; do not be dismayed, for I am your God. I will strengthen you and help you; I will uphold you with my righteous right hand (Isaiah 41:10).

Years earlier when our second son David was born, my joy could not be contained as he was given to me in the hospital. He has been a loving addition to our family from the minute he was born. He was sweet, innocent, and loved beyond words. He was like a clean slate and had endless potential as life began. I was excited to be a part of his life, and I prayed for guidance to help him enjoy its wonderment.

In the early stages of David's development, his mother and I had no indication he was different than any other baby. He had bright blue eyes, blond hair, and a smile that would melt your heart. Developmentally, his motor skills were right on track. He sat, crawled, and walked all within the normal age range. As a matter of fact, he outpaced his brothers in some areas. Our concern centered on his inability to talk. His speech was extremely delayed. At his three-year pediatric visit, David's speech delay was a growing concern. We were advised to wait six months, and if he did not begin talking by then, we were to bring him back for further testing. After six months, there was still no change in his verbal ability, so we were referred to several specialists for follow-up. At three and a half years old, he was diagnosed with a form of autism.

Although David did not speak, it was obvious he was an intelligent little guy. His sweetness was evident at an early age. When his little brother, Stephen, was born, he would bring him a toy or blanket when he started to cry. When David wanted a drink of water or juice, he used a kitchen chair to climb on the counter and held out an empty cup until someone filled it for him. His favorite book was Green Eggs and Ham, and he wore out three copies. When he wanted someone to read to him, he got the book and his favorite yellow blanket and sat on the couch until someone complied. The rituals he established provided comfort and order in his world.

His mother and I began to see a pattern emerging in his behaviors. He retreated emotionally when the stimulus from his environment became overwhelming. He ignored us when we tried to refocus his attention on a current activity. He acted as if he could not hear, and I began wondering if he were deaf. He preferred to repeat previously learned activities continually and was uninterested in trying new things.

David became interested in simple puzzles. He spent a great deal of time trying to fit the large pieces together in a six-piece puzzle. It was difficult to help him assemble these puzzles because his speech delay prevented him from communicating with me, and his cognitive skills were uncertain. He also liked multicolored blocks with bright colors. I used these blocks to devise a simple game. I tossed a few different-colored blocks on the floor and asked him to bring me a specific color. If he brought the wrong color, I would not accept it as he handed it to me, but if he brought the correct color, I praised him. It did not take long for him to understand the concept of the game, and he ultimately learned his colors.

Our pediatrician suggested we take advantage of any available early social opportunities. He thought preschool would help David immensely, so we enrolled him. In his first year, he added a few words to his vocabulary and learned to answer simple questions with a yes or no. As preschool came to an end in the spring, we looked for options to keep him engaged with other children.

In the fall, we decided to enroll him in kindergarten in the public school system. With the help of a full-time paraprofessional, David was the first autistic child to be mainstreamed into the general education curriculum in the Oxford school district. David struggled to complete class assignments, and we believed his speech delay was the root cause of his academic issues.

David's language barrier affected him in every aspect of childhood development, preventing him from forming friendships and blending in with his classmates. Children initiated conversations with him in an effort to make friends; however, when he did not respond, they usually turned to other friends, and he was left alone.

David's inability to communicate with other children broke my heart. Each moment of silence built a barrier that grew daily, isolating him from others. As the years passed, the barrier was so high, he no longer believed he could overcome it. He lost hope of ever forming friendships at school.

Throughout his childhood, David's two brothers were the friends he relied upon. He retreated to the familiar surroundings of his family. However, he still preferred independent activities and seemed happy playing in his own little world. He loved to run, swing, play video games, watch Star Trek, and create works of art on the driveway with sidewalk chalk. He drew maps of the streets in the subdivision and created video game levels.

David had a great deal of energy and was constantly on the move. We looked for ways to make him happy. One of the things he enjoyed was walking behind the tractor in the paths of freshly mowed grass. We cut mazes in the lawn, and he was content for days, walking along the paths and humming the Star Trek theme song.

Some of David's first memories were of great family vacations. He was four years old when we went to Florida. He remembers being on a Star Trek set at Universal Studios. The entire family was dressed in Star Trek uniforms, with the exception of his younger brother, Stephen, who was very young and still in a stroller. We went into a room with several chairs and a blank green screen.

Television sets hung from the ceiling, and cue cards

Michael, Todd, and David

were posted on the wall. We were instructed to look directly at the cards and read them aloud when the attendants pointed to them. David was fascinated with the televisions as the movie played. I enjoyed watching his reaction to the video. His eyes were wide open with amazement as the movie placed him in the scene.

David often refers to the world around him in a literal way. On our family vacation to Mount Rushmore, he called the national landmark "four faces on a rock." When we referred to Mount Rushmore, he did not understand what we were talking about. We began using "four faces on a rock" in many of our conversations about that vacation so as to include him.

When David returned to school in the fall, he explained he had been to four faces on a rock in South Dakota. His teacher thought that was hysterical and laughed about it for the longest time. We had a t-shirt made for her with a picture of Mount Rushmore and the caption, "Four Faces on a Rock." I understand she cherished the shirt for many years.

David has one tragic memory that he will never forget. David was nearing his eleventh birthday. He received a note from the school office, stating he was not to take the bus home that afternoon, as was his normal routine. The teachers made sure both he and Stephen were rerouted to the proper classroom for the after-school program. David knew something was wrong but was unable to express his concerns. Both he and Stephen waited patiently for someone to pick them up from school and bring them home.

Our subdivision had one entrance and one road that connected to a series of cul-de-sacs. A close friend of the family arrived at the school and took both boys to her home, which was located just a few doors beyond our house. David thought it was strange when she drove past his home without stopping. He noticed all the cars parked in our driveway, as well as a dozen along the roadside. At the neighbor's house, both boys played video games and had fun while they waited for us to pick them up.

When David and Stephen returned home, the house was filled with people. David was confused when he saw the familiar faces of his aunts and uncles. As he headed for the stairs, he heard someone say, "He was a really good guy." In the upstairs bedroom, we waited to share the news of the family tragedy that had taken place earlier in the day.

When David entered the master bedroom with Stephen, his mother and I struggled to find the words no parent should ever have to deliver. My heart was absolutely crushed and broken. Anna and I did our best to compose ourselves enough to be sensitive to the needs of our remaining children. Anna told both boys that their brother had died. They cried for a long time. I do not know how fully they understood the concept of death. They did know Michael would never talk to them or play with them again. Their oldest brother, whom they idolized, was gone forever.

~ 6 ~

The Silent Cry

For the grave cannot praise you, death cannot sing your praise; those who go down to the pit cannot hope for your faithfulness. The living, the living—they praise you, as I am doing today; parents tell their children about your faithfulness (Isaiah 38:18-19).

The news and realization of the permanence of Michael's death shattered the entire family. Privately, we were all devastated and did not know how to process our emotions. I could not reconcile his loss on any level. Each of us suffered in silence, stunned by the revelation. That day, we joined the ranks of many grieving families touched by adolescent suicide.

Anna and I took our remaining sons to counseling to help them deal with their feelings. No words can describe how a heart can break or a spirit can be crushed when facing this type of reality. Michael's death left a huge hole in our hearts. Years later, the scars from his sudden passing still remain in each of us as we remember that horrific day.

The loss of his brother intensified David's emotional struggles. He was unable to cope with his daily battle with autism and feelings of grief. He began experiencing random panic attacks at school, which caused his body to feel shaky inside and created confusion in his brain. He complained about his forehead hurting when these episodes occurred. To this day, he does not like to remember those torrents of pain in his head.

We had hoped seventh grade would provide a fresh start for David. But new issues arose as the elevated noise levels in hallways and in the lunchroom provided yet another nemesis. Noise always distracted him, and background noise made it hard for him to focus in class. That year proved to be yet another disappointment for him. By the end of seventh grade, David knew he was different from his classmates. He tried to fit in, but he lacked the social skills and the confidence needed to make friends. The more he tried to be social, the more anxious he became, resulting in more panic attacks. In time, this repetitious cycle created feelings of depression. His self-image was redefined as that of failure. He felt as if everything in life were closing in on him, and he was powerless over his circumstances.

David calls eighth grade his year of hell. He experienced moderate to severe panic attacks about twice a week that year. He struggled to fit in socially, and it was hard for him to initiate conversation. The noise issues continued to torment him, making it difficult for him to concentrate. He also had a lot more homework.

His mother and I tutored him throughout the evening hours. Often, his pace was slow and there was too much work for him to do. Most nights, he worked on his assignments until it was time to go to bed. When the alarm clock went off in the morning, he was still exhausted from the night before. This ritual continued on a daily basis until Anna met with the school principal, and together they agreed to lighten his course load.

Anna talked to David about trying out for the cross-country team. He had tried other sports in the past, like street hockey and basketball, but he couldn't grasp the team concept. Cross-country allowed him to participate with a group without having the close social interdependence. He loved to run and we thought cross-country might be good for him.

David had a slender build and was a storehouse of physical energy, a perfect combination for a runner. At the beginning of eighth grade, he joined the team. At first, he was not able to run the entire distance without walking part way. David practiced diligently, and by the second team meet, he could run the entire race. Participating in cross-country gave him a sense of euphoria, as the physical activity of running helped clear his head.

When the eighth grade school year ended, David joined a cross-country summer program and ran at a local park. He trained in the heat of the summer months. Often the team swam in a local lake after the grueling practice. David absolutely loved this ritual. While he was not one of the fastest runners on the team, he was the fastest swimmer. He felt included and connected to his teammates as he raced in the water. Cross-country and track helped him to begin to socialize with his peers.

In his freshman year of high school, David enthusiastically joined the track and cross-country teams. His prior experiences in the sports were positive, and he was passionate about running. Throughout his high school years, his athletic experience formed the basis of understanding the dynamics of a team. He tried to integrate into the team's social environment, but his lack of social skills continued to plague him

30

each and every season. Over time, he learned that running was a great way to combat the feelings of confusion caused by his autism.

Academically, David struggled in all areas of comprehension, and his writing skills suffered. Although he could not master even the simplest story problem, his math skills were exceptional and his favorite subject was pre-calculus. It became somewhat embarrassing for me when I could no longer help him with his math assignments. I had a bachelor's degree in business administration from a respected university, and he surpassed my knowledge of the subject in his senior year. Anna and I helped him with his homework several hours each night, trying to give him a fighting chance to achieve his goals after high school.

David was becoming an adult in a world that is often unkind to people with disabilities. We tried our best to prepare him for the journey awaiting him. Our thoughts focused on the security issues of life, questions like, How will our son support himself? What type of job will he be able to hold? Will he be able to live on his own? Will he fall in love? What will he do when we are gone? These are the questions most parents dwell upon when looking to the future. Knowing the world can be a cruel place, we had to find a way to help him improve his social skills so he could blend with others in society.

After high school, David's social fears and problems intensified in his new and unknown environments, which led to depression. Each time he failed to talk to someone, he reasoned that they did not want to talk to him because he was ugly. He constantly reinforced this mantra, which greatly added to his issues and intensified his negative self-image.

David was traveling in a downward, pessimistic spiral, viewing the glass as half empty. As he went through each day, he saw the worst-case scenario in every event. For example, if a thunderstorm was forecasted, he immediately began deciding what he would do when the house was swept away by a tornado. He saw everything in his life as negative, and he reveled in it.

David was cynical and always expected bad things to happen, which became a self-fulfilling prophecy. His negative mindset snowballed to other aspects of his life as well. He became frustrated with the simplest unfinished tasks and called himself stupid for not completing them properly. He was a perfectionist without the skills needed for perfection. He lived in his own kind of hell. It was heartbreaking to watch.

David not only suffered from autism but also depression, grief, and uncertainty. He plunged into the depths of despair, and I was concerned his depression might lead him to make the same terrible mistake his brother Michael had made. I could see him struggle as he watched other people his age moving forward in life, enjoying friendships, and making plans for college. His social isolation was at a crisis point.

David vented his frustrations on a punching bag I had set up for him in the basement. He put on boxing gloves to protect his hands from the abrasiveness of the one-hundred-pound bag. He wailed on the bag until he could no longer hold up his arms. I always knew when he was having a bad day because when he walked in the house, he immediately went into the basement to punch the bag. I listened for him to get worn out before I tried to intervene. By then, the intensity of the physical strain had calmed him enough to process my words and work through his problems.

One of the worst feelings a father can have is the inability to help his child. I spent countless hours trying to help David see the world differently. Each conversation was similar: he would get upset about a situation he had just encountered and would attach personal meaning to the event in an unhealthy way. I tried to help him deal with his frustrations in a logical and rational manner. For several minutes, he would calm down and listen as I spoke, but when I finished speaking, he often reverted to the same negative thinking. It was as if he played the same record over and over again in his mind.

I had one strategy for dealing with his temper if a punching bag was not available—I intervened with humor and laughter. If I could get him to smile or laugh (even a little), his anger reset button would activate, and he would be fine.

One evening, David dropped a dinner plate, shattering it on the kitchen floor. He became angry with himself and started down the road of self-pity. His anger boiled over as he blamed his autistic tendencies for his loss of temper. I noticed the dishware he dropped was of the nearly unbreakable type, and I told him the plate should not have broken by just dropping it. I tried to get him to listen to reason. He was spiraling out of control emotionally when I had an ingenious idea. I grabbed a bowl from the same set of dishware, in an attempt to demonstrate how it was not supposed to break. I spent a minute or two pontificating about the strength and resilience of this dishware. I dropped the bowl in the middle of the kitchen and (you guessed it) it shattered all over the floor. We laughed hard as the floor was covered with the broken shards of our plate and bowl. The laughter broke his self-imposed punishment. I made a mental note to buy a lot more of this type of dinnerware, because it could come in handy when we needed to laugh.

I have learned never to underestimate the value and power of laughter. It gives David the opportunity to pause and enjoy the simple ironies of life. I have successfully incorporated this strategy as a way to de-escalate many of the minor difficulties of life.

David's passions for geography and astronomy have also truly been a godsend. He studies maps of the world and foreign countries and is fascinated with the stars and the universe. Years ago, I purchased a powerful telescope, which he uses to increase his knowledge of the solar system. I have spent many evenings viewing the planets with him. He has taught me a lot about astronomy. He has an uncanny ability to locate the planets in the night sky. In fact, he has a phone app that gives real-time data about the location of the planets and star formations, so he can have up-to-the-minute information.

After high school, David enrolled in a local university, where he experienced difficulty passing basic classes. He was determined to press on, but each new class brought additional frustration. He became angry as he fell behind. I feared that many of his future prospects for employment were slipping away as he dropped out of class after class.

While all his peers pursued their education, he couldn't choose a vocation. Each unsuccessful class reinforced his negative self-image. His depression intensified as his world collapsed around him. Our family spent countless hours encouraging him to continue with his schooling. Fortunately, he listened to our advice and did not give up on his education.

At age twenty, David was an intelligent and handsome young man with bright blue eyes and sandy brown hair. His autistic traits were somewhat apparent in his behaviors, but his social fears continued to drive him to avoid conversation. His lack of personal interaction with his peers inhibited any chance of forming positive relationships. He was keenly aware of his emotional differences and tried his best to hide his inability to communicate effectively. To the outside world, he appeared shy. But inwardly, he viewed his silence as an ongoing failure and therefore referred to himself as ugly and stupid.

David

For most of his life, David's dreams were limited by his autism. However, one objective remained strong in his heart. He wanted someday to attend the University of Michigan. Academically, he had a lot of work to do to attain his goal. We never fully understood his affection toward U of M, considering we did not have any particular family allegiance toward the school. Throughout his childhood, his preferred wardrobe was maize and blue. As the story progresses, you will understand why, to this day, he loves their football team and enthusiastically cheers them on.

~ 7 ~

Life Is a Tapestry

For he was looking forward to the city with foundations, whose architect and builder is God (Hebrews 11:10).

Although I was still working full-time at General Motors, the dream of ministry began to rekindle in my heart. For years, I had talked with Anna about entering the ministry, and I believed our marriage was relatively stable and would be enhanced by the new direction. The United States was ten months post 9-11 when I enrolled at Michigan Theological Seminary. I planned to finish my seminary training before I retired from the automaker. This opportunity was like a second chance to fulfill a lifelong calling to serve God.

Just as the landscape of the country changed in the blink of an eye, my life would also experience rapid change. Anna and I struggled as a couple. Again, I thought our conflict was relatively minor. Our unresolved differences solidified over time until we could no longer function as a loving couple. I felt as if we had wasted our second chance, as divorce once again became our reality. The entire tapestry of my life unraveled before me. With our family falling apart once again, I needed God to fashion my life differently.

On a cool autumn morning, as part of an assignment for a

spiritual formation class, I cleared my mind and for
the beauty of nature as I listened for the still, small voice of
God. I found a bench at the end of a boat dock at a pic-
turesque county park and surveyed the lake in front of me.
The wind was absent so the lake was calm and looked like
glass. I sat motionless on the bench, gazing across the lake. It
was the perfect setting for my assignment. I felt as if God had
pulled up a chair for me so I could experience His presence. I
watched and waited for inspiration.

I had a notebook and pen in hand but didn't know what
to write. I felt somewhat silly and vulnerable, seeking God in
this way. Usually, I gave Him a laundry list of items that were
on my mind, but today I waited to see what was on His
mind. I knew I needed to relax and clear my thoughts. After
spending time in reflection and prayer, I looked across the
water. The view from my vantage point was amazingly beautiful. The far shore reflected on the water like a mirror, offering me a spectacular sight. I noticed a small maple leaf
floating on the water close to me. The air was completely
still. I watched the leaf as it moved about slowly. It turned
from side to side and changed directions ever so slightly in
the water. For a moment, I wondered if its movements had a
purpose. Perhaps this was part of a journey the gentle wind
was guiding.

I tracked the movement of this small, insignificant leaf
for some time. Subtle motions moved it farther from the
shoreline. A western wind could immediately end its journey
on the lake by carrying it to the shore. However, since there
was no wind, it remained on the lake. It occurred to me that I
was on a journey, much like the leaf, and I wanted God's
Spirit to guide me. In the stillness, I realized my life was a

mixture of driving winds interrupted by brief moments of serenity. It was time for my life to begin again in the peacefulness of His presence.

Like the leaf upon the water, God was intervening in my life. My journey at Michigan Theological Seminary seemed much like a double-edged sword. I had the opportunity to restart a long-awaited calling; however, Anna and I could not make our marriage work. Our second chance for a unified family failed. I knew being divorced would be a difficult obstacle to overcome in a pursuit of a pastoral position.

The Bible tells us that God's ways are not our ways. I knew I had to push forward and prepare for an unknown calling of some type. This time I was ready to comply fully with the work God had for me. I was willing to trust Him and move forward, believing my path would lead to greater light. I knew if darkness encompassed me on the journey, God would find me anyway.

Three years had passed from the time of my divorce. I continued working full-time, attending seminary, and spending as much time as I could with my two boys. In 2006, while in my last semester, I planned to travel to the Holy Land to visit the historical sites mentioned in the Bible. I asked my friend Renee if she too wanted to travel with our group.

The study tour to Israel would give Renee an incredible spiritual experience as she saw the Bible from the perspective of a picture book. This invitation was nothing more than an innocent gesture to include her in this adventure, since our relationship was casual. I told her she would be assigned a roommate from among the women in the group. She was excited to be given the opportunity to participate in such an in-depth Bible study tour in the land of Israel.

Visiting the Holy Land felt like going home. I had read about the remarkable places in the Bible from early childhood, but I never imagined traveling there. I was thrilled at the opportunity to participate with fellow students. At the airport, Renee met her new roommate and quickly made friends. The flight left Detroit and stopped briefly in Germany as we switched planes to continue non-stop to Tel-Aviv, Israel.

I will never forget the trip to Israel. It was perfect on many levels. After leaving the valley known as Armageddon, we traveled to the northern region called Tel Dan. When God divided up the land of Israel, He gave portions to the twelve sons of Jacob (Israel). Of these twelve sons, Dan received the northernmost portions. Centuries earlier, God had instructed Abraham to walk the land, and He promised to give him and his descendants all the ground that his foot touched. Tel Dan is the first place in the Promised Land that Abraham's foot would have touched.

Tel Dan

39

Standing on the northern shore overlooking the Sea of Galilee was inspirational. On ancient shores, the Sermon on the Mount came to life in a powerful way. In my heart, the echoes from the sea fed my soul as the whispers of Jesus touched my mind. I longed to spend as much time as possible in the places where Jesus walked and performed miracles.

Tiberius is a city on the western side of the Sea of Galilee. It offers a breathtaking view of the northern shore and is a place of significant remembrance for me. One evening, just after dinner, I was walking with Renee on a boardwalk that overlooks the Sea of Galilee. The sky was calm and the sea tranquil. We looked to the north, where small, flickering lights from the hillside reflected on the water. We watched them as they sparkled across the land-scape like the stars of heaven. I thought about the signifi-cance of the lights from the distant town and wondered if we were looking at the same one Jesus spoke about when He said, "A town built on a hill cannot be hidden" (Matthew 5:14b).

Soon the flickering lights became a blur as tears welled up in my eyes. My tears intensified as my childhood memories flashed before me when I could feel God's presence all around. Have you ever experienced a perfect moment? I knew with every fiber of my being that I was in the midst of one. I loved being in that moment, and I wish I could have stayed there forever. I wanted to immortalize every detail of the set-ting. Renee too could feel the presence of God in that place and, together on the shores of Galilee, we shared a great spir-itual epiphany. I asked her to help me always remember and honor the treasure we found at Galilee.

We returned to our group, which was still gathered at the

dinner table, and shared our experience with them. One by one, they crossed the boulevard and came to the boardwalk. The presence of God was still evident in the serenity and beauty of the night air. There was a sense of awe in those who came as they too viewed the beauty of Galilee with their heart's eye.

We spent the next day touring Capernaum and Bethsaida and sailing on a wooden boat on the sea. Galilee once again left an indelible mark on my soul as the rustic boat floated silently on the waters Christ once walked upon. As we continued our journey, Renee and I were baptized in the Jordan River.

Jerusalem was a special treat, as a plethora of Bible stories flooded my mind. I stood in awe in the ancient room where Jesus celebrated the Last Supper with His disciples. This fourth-century building was reconstructed upon the ruins of the sacred and holy site. For me, it is the greatest room in the entire world. At this location, Jesus took the bread and the wine and gave it to His disciples: "This is my

Door to the Upper Room

blood of the covenant, which is poured out for many for the forgiveness of sins. I tell you, I will not drink from this fruit of the vine from now on until that day when I drink it new with you in my Father's kingdom" (Matthew 26:28-29).

41

Finally at Jerusalem's Wailing Wall (the Western Wall), I prayed for my family and for direction in ministry. The wall was constructed to protect the city and the temple in Jerusalem. Today, it is all that remains of a 3000-year-old temple that once housed the Ark of the Covenant and the presence of God. Jesus taught in this temple and predicted its destruction. Every day, people place prayers like mortar into the cracks in the wall, hoping God will one day answer. Likewise, this trip served to invigorate the passion of the child in me and allowed me to regain an age-old dream.

Wailing Wall with the messages tucked into the crevices

Traveling in the Holy Land was a special time for me. The Sea of Galilee enriched and beckoned my soul. I think about this trip and my feelings associated with Galilee quite often. Standing in the Holy Land was like the second half of my encounter with God, which began in my backyard when I was nine years old.

After this experience, I began to view Renee as a kind and sweet soul mate of incredible value. She is beautiful, caring, empathic, and compassionate. She has a great enthusiasm for life and adventure. She is tenderhearted and optimistic, with a great passion for God. She has many character traits I admire. Soon I began to notice that her smile had the power to light up my heart whenever she was near.

The tapestry of my life started to come together. In December 2007, Renee and I were given second chances at love and life. We were married on the one-year anniversary of our trip to Israel. We are a blended family, with her two sons and my two sons.

I continued working at General Motors with thirty-one years to my credit. I had finished seminary training and prepared for ministry after finishing my career at GM. The events that would transpire in February 2009 would give me the urgency to retire at last and begin a new journey following a decades-old dream. I was fortunate to have a beautiful wife who shared my dreams and goals. We were both ready for the next phase of service to God. I felt as if we were clay in the hands of a great potter as He prepared us for destinations unknown.

~ 8 ~

When Disaster Strikes

When you pass through the waters, I will be with you; and when you pass through the rivers, they will not sweep over you. When you walk through the fire, you will not be burned; the flames will not set you ablaze (Isaiah 43:2).

On Friday, February 20, 2009, David felt ill and left his part-time job as a bagger at Kroger. He was feverish and felt sick to his stomach. Renee and I initially thought he was experiencing the early symptoms of the flu. His condition did not improve through the night, and his fever increased. On Saturday morning, I took him to our local urgent care facility. He developed a rash, which started on his chest and slowly spread over his entire body. The doctor's original diagnosis was strep throat. He gave him medication and sent him home.

On Sunday, his condition continued to deteriorate. He had a 103-degree fever, and the rash covered his body like intense sunburn. I took him back to the same urgent care facility where he had been treated the previous day. On this visit, he was diagnosed and treated for scarlet fever. The doctor stated it was a classic case. He was given different medication and sent home. As Sunday night gave way to Monday morning, he became lethargic and his temperature rose to 103.5.

On Monday, David's condition continued to worsen. His mother, Anna, and I took him to the emergency room at Troy Beaumont Hospital. He was admitted to the hospital and observed that day and night without a diagnosis. On Tuesday, specialists were consulted but could not determine the source of his illness. He developed huge water blisters on every part of his body. The doctors were stumped at the underlying cause of these massive sores.

An infectious-disease specialist consulted with a staff dermatologist, who finally gave a correct diagnosis. Although he had never encountered a patient with this uncommon affliction, David's symptoms were spot on. The diagnosis was Stevens-Johnson Syndrome (SJS) and Toxic Epidermal Necrolysis (TEN). SJS and TEN are two forms of a life-threatening skin condition in which cell death causes the epidermis to separate from the dermis.

The doctor told me if David didn't get advanced care immediately, he would not survive. He gave me two options: the University of Michigan Hospital in Ann Arbor or Detroit Receiving Hospital. David's preference was obvious to me. The emergency preparations were made for his transportation on the Survival Flight helicopter from Troy to U of M Hospital.

This diagnosis of SJS and TEN was absolutely devastating to us. I still remember the feeling of urgency as we waited for the helicopter to land. As David sat in bed, waiting for the Survival Flight transport, large quantities of liquid collected under his skin, forming multiple blisters on his body. The first one was near his Adam's apple. It appeared to have at least a quarter of a cup of liquid in it and was about five inches in diameter. He looked much like a bullfrog as the skin sagged from the weight of the water. On David's arm appeared a larger sore, perhaps six inches in diameter and holding even more liquid. His skin was bubbling up on every area of his torso. These pockets of fluid occasionally ruptured, prevented him from lying back against the bed. He sat upright in an effort to minimize the breaking of the skin that caused intense pain. His fever had been above 103 degrees for more than four days, and he was shivering violently from his current fever of 104.5.

I called my wife, Renee, and other family members with the news. The phone calls were brief because I didn't want to leave David for any length of time. I told my family David was being airlifted to U of M in Ann Arbor and he was going to be admitted to the Burn Trauma Center.

I helplessly watched as a Survival Flight helicopter carried my son into the dark night sky. His life was quickly waning, his skin separating from his body. Time seemed to stand still as he disappeared into the starlight. In that horrific moment, I wondered if I would ever see my son alive again.

David arrived at U of M Hospital on Tuesday evening. My sister Joan and brother-in-law Larry managed to meet the helicopter as it landed. I received a call from them while Renee and I were still on the road. We arrived about forty minutes later, as did David's mother, Anna.

The trauma team ran a battery of tests on David to determine what actions could stabilize his condition. The entire outer layer of his skin was falling off, which made it impossible to run IV lines for fluids and medication. Without this access, he would not survive long. The doctors rushed him into surgery to insert a central line in his neck. This procedure was risky for him, but time was of the essence if we wanted to see him alive again. This operation was his only chance to survive. If it failed, he would die. Having no other choice, I signed the paperwork.

The waiting room for the burn trauma unit was just outside the electronic doors that led to the ICU. We stayed in this room the first night, waiting for further news on the outcome of the surgery and David's condition. The room was small, approximately ten feet by fifteen feet, with a desk, computer, and phone. The furniture was uncomfortable and the florescent lights could not be turned off. There were no windows in the room, and the walls were white. It gave me a claustrophobic feeling, much like a doctor's examination room. I felt trapped as we waited for updates. David was about a hundred feet away from us in the ICU, and there was nothing we could do except wait.

We waited well into the early morning hours and finally learned that the central line had been inserted successfully. David survived two huge hurdles that night: the helicopter trip to the hospital and the insertion of the central line. This was the beginning of a long road for him.

Fear gripped my heart as my second son fought for his life. My mind flashed back ten years, and I was horrified as I remembered the intense pain of losing my oldest son. This day was sending chills down my spine again, and I felt I could not escape certain doom. I had learned to dislike everything about February, and I was grateful it was the shortest month. Most years, I experience twenty-eight days of anxiety, regret, anger, and depression. Ten years earlier, Michael had died on the very same date. Each year, as this anniversary approached, I suffered in silence as the memory of Michael's life filled my heart with sadness. The wound caused by his death was deep and paralyzed my soul. Every day of the month served as a reminder that the nightmare of losing a son had not ended.

The next morning was coincidently also Ash Wednesday, a time of repentance and reflection upon mortality. On that day, I did not view Ash Wednesday in a religious sense, but I did feel as if my life were turning to ashes as I focused on David's welfare. In the back of my mind, I was terrified of losing my second son. I remember someone saying, "God, please don't let him die on this day," to which I replied, "God, don't let him die on any day."

The hospital tests confirmed the diagnosis of SJS TEN. All his skin was falling off his body, and he was in extreme pain. He cried out in agony as one blister after another popped and discarded the now-dead skin. His prognosis was poor. He had the worst case of SJS TEN the hospital had ever encountered. The odds of a rash of this nature expanding to a full-blown case of SJS TEN are more than one in a million. For some reason, David was the one. But this would not be the first time he beat the long odds. When David was born, the autism rate in infants was 1 in 25,000.

I wondered if the nightmare of February 25 had re-appeared to claim my second son. My thoughts tormented me as I walked the corridors in a misty darkness of despair. The tempests of death seemed to rage around David, and I felt absolutely helpless. David seemed to be moments from death, and I could do nothing about it. The irony of this event on this day horrified me beyond words.

David was at death's door as the doctors reported on the extent of his illness. Sloughing is the technical term for the shedding of skin. In addition to his external skin loss, David's body was now sloughing internally as he lost tissue in his mouth, trachea, and lungs. At this early stage, there was no way to predict how far the internal sloughing would spread. His liver was not functioning correctly, and his 103-104.5 fever continued. His heart rate was 150-160 beats per minute, which far exceeded the normal 60-100 beats per minute, putting a tremendous strain on his heart. Because the skin is considered the largest organ of the human body, David's massive skin loss, coupled with his deteriorating liver, meant he was in multiple organ failure.

We asked the doctors what options were available to him. Initially, they told us he had been placed on a liver transplant list. Shortly thereafter, we learned he was removed from the list because it was unlikely he would survive the surgery. All the medical data indicated he would not survive any operation at this point. The doctors gave us some hope of the liver regaining function on its own. This news came at a price, as they could not give him certain types of pain medication because they would further compromise his liver function. This meant his suffering could not be relieved with medicine, and his pain would be more intense as his skin fell off his body.

The director of one of the clinical research departments talked to my wife and me about placing David into a liver study. I was so overtaken with grief and emotion that I was not able to understand her intent. I believed she had an ulterior motive for offering this study. I knew the hospital engaged in teaching activities, studies, and cutting-edge procedures; however, I did not want to agree to any intervention that would further compromise his condition. In the back of my mind, I was hoping entrance into a study group would mean additional and perhaps unusual measures might be available to him. I reluctantly agreed to the study.

Although David's wounds were not from a burn, the treatment was similar. Infection was a major concern because of the skin loss. His wounds needed to be cleaned and the dead skin removed. Then the staff would bandage his entire body to protect him from germs and infection. As the loose skin was removed, his pleading screams pierced my soul. I couldn't bear it as he cried for help and begged them to stop. It was as if my child were being tortured right in front of me and I could do nothing to help him. I have never felt so utterly helpless.

Finally, I could no longer take the stress of his pleadings. In that horrible moment, it felt as if my soul were dying. I couldn't cope with my circumstances for another minute, but I hated leaving David in his desperate state. Renee struggled to keep me standing as we walked down the hallway. I was in a place where I had never been before. I believe God drove me out of the room. I needed to go to a place where my spirit could be protected.

We walked toward the main lobby. I needed time away from the horror to regroup my thoughts and overcome the intense fear of the moment. In the lobby stood a small showcase approximately ten feet by six feet, depicting a doctor's office in the early days of modern medicine. I looked at the room enclosed by glass, safe from the contamination of the outside world. I wanted to break the seal of the enclosed office and live in this safe shelter, pretending I was merely having a bad dream. I looked again at the doctor's office on display and told my wife that on February 25, 2019, I would lock my third son, Stephen, in the glass case to protect him from this day. This day was like a curse to me. I wondered if the pain from my past nightmare combined with the pain of my current situation could ever be redeemed. The significance of the ten-year anniversary of Michael's death played over and over in my mind. I could almost see an image of David's gravestone alongside Michael's, both displaying the same date. This absolutely tormented me. David was struggling just down the hallway, and I could not help him any more than I could help my son Michael. What I needed was a second chance to avoid the pain and suffering that February 25 brought to my life. If I could only turn back time ten years, I could be in the right place at the right time and could avoid certain disaster. Unfortunately, this type of second chance is not available in this world. Neither can an isolated glass room protect anyone from life's circumstances.

~ 9 ~

The Difficult Road

We are hard pressed on every side, but not crushed; perplexed, but not in despair; persecuted, but not abandoned; struck down, but not destroyed (2 Corinthians 4:8-9).

David was placed on a ventilator because the lining of his lungs was detaching, and he needed assistance to breathe. The process included drawing the sloughed tissue out of his lungs while the ventilator functioned. It was ghastly to watch as they suctioned the tissue from his lungs so he could continue to receive the oxygen needed to keep him alive.

David was motionless and on a ventilator for several days. The monitor showed an elevated heart rate of 150-160 beats per minute. Tachycardia is a condition that occurs when the heart is beating above 100 beats per minute at rest. There are a variety of reasons for the body to increase blood flow throughout the system. Many of these are temporary in nature and do not pose long-term risks. However, if left unmonitored and untreated, this can become life-threatening. David had a distinct advantage that would prove vital in dealing with his elevated heart rate: long-distance running had strengthened his cardiovascular system, minimizing the chances that tachycardia would complicate his condition further. He was in great physical shape. The doctors said his age and physical conditioning would greatly increase his chances of survival, because his heart would be more likely to withstand the strain.

The list of nightmare scenarios continued on a daily basis. There were many tense hours following news updates, as lab reports were made available to us. It was hard to prioritize every concern flooding his way. He was truly in survival mode, struggling to live. The secondary cascading health issues seemed distant to us because his recovery was still uncertain.

The amazing medical team at U of M took a proactive approach to David's treatment. Not only did they hastily address his current symptoms, but they also made preparations for the additional symptoms that had not appeared yet. An ophthalmologist was added to the care team to proactively address the significant scarring that was predicted to take place under his eyelids as a result of SJS TEN. We were told everything was being done to protect David's cornea from being scratched by the scar tissue on the interior of his eyelids as the skin peeled away.

David was taken to the operating room to sew membranes onto his eyeball. These membranes served as a barrier between his cornea and his eyelid. Again, I was called on to give permission for his surgery. I asked if this surgery was absolutely necessary. The thought of stitching his eyeball turned my stomach. The doctors explained that his cornea was being scratched by scar tissue under his eyelid. This membrane would function as a barrier and a Band-Aid of flesh to protect his cornea. Many SJS patients lose their sight if the scar tissue under the eyelid carves ridges in the cornea.

We asked our family and friends to add David to the

prayer lists at their churches. We also enlisted several area congregations to begin praying for him. It was extremely difficult to share the scope of the problem with those who were interceding on his behalf because he had so many physical issues. I prioritized a prayer list and gave various worship centers the significant health issues to pray for. Thousands of people prayed for David's recovery.

David was experiencing total liver failure. He desperately needed to regain some liver function to stay alive. The nursing staff tested his blood frequently to monitor the condition of his liver. The results of these tests indicated the severity of deterioration. His liver numbers were between 4,000 and 5,000 and they needed to get below 200 for normal function. If these statistics failed to get radically lower quickly, he would most likely die.

The next day, David's liver function had marginally improved. I hoped he would live long enough to give his system a fighting chance to recover from his ailing liver. His test results had a value above 3,000 for two days. With each test, we saw a small improvement of 30 to 80 points. We asked everyone we knew to pray for his liver function to return. Miraculously, the numbers improved dramatically. On the third day, his results showed an 800-point reduction from the night before. The furious liver storm blew over as quickly as it had arrived. The next two days brought intense relief as his liver numbers dropped into the 200-300 range. His liver function was no longer a life-threatening concern. However, a second, more deadly hurdle still remained.

The skin is a protective membrane used to isolate our internal organs from infection and disease. Without this protection, any small infectious agent could potentially end an already-compromised person's life. David's external skin had peeled off his body in large pieces as the water blisters popped. The skin that remained was also falling off in large sections. The outer layers of skin on his entire right foot came off in one piece, looking much like rubber goulashes worn over dress shoes. Without the protection of his external skin, infection could quickly overtake him with deadly results.

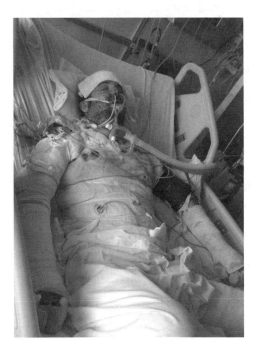

David's life had transformed into a mini-hell. He was in constant agony as the nerve endings were exposed to room air without the buffer that skin provides. The pain was excruciating as these raw nerves sent messages to the brain. The very air, which gives life, now brought incomprehensible pain. The thought of what he was going through frightened me beyond belief. Consider for a minute the protective skin on your body is completely missing. The nerves relaying messages to the brain are still intact; however, they are now exposed to outside air. Have you ever had a small patch of skin missing, perhaps on your finger? Can you remember the amount of pain it caused? Everyone at one time or another has experienced the agony of missing the top layer of skin and having water or air come in contact with it. Most can recall the pain vividly. Imagine every square centimeter of your body having an injury in which the outer skin was gone. This was the situation David had to endure because he was missing all of his skin.

It was vitally important for David's body to regenerate his external skin quickly. The hospital staff made every effort to achieve this goal. His bandaged body needed a tremendous amount of nutrition and calories. A feeding tube was inserted directly into his stomach thru his nose. He received 5,000 to 6,000 calories per day through the feeding tube in an effort to supply his body with enough calories to undertake the enormous task of growing new skin. The regrowth of his epidermis was now the highest priority on the prayer list. If he could regenerate his outer layer before an infection set in, his chances for survival would increase dramatically.

~ 10 ~

Tormented!

As he went along, he saw a man blind from birth. His disciples asked him, "Rabbi, who sinned, this man or his parents, that he was born blind?" "Neither this man nor his parents sinned," said Jesus, "but this happened so that the works of God might be displayed in him" (John 9:1-3).

How often do we think suffering is the judgment of God? People can be cruel and judgmental when they insinuate God is repaying you for some past sin. We will all have times of trials. Knowing the specific reason for our troubles has eluded mankind for millennia. When my oldest son, Michael, died ten years earlier, I looked for answers to this tragedy and could find none. The lack of answers served only to torment my mind with thoughts of why me? Neither could I find comfort in the scriptures. I felt as if I were cursed by the ongoing events in my life.

Eventually I would discover the truths of Psalm 139:16. This psalm speaks of God's knowledge of us. Before we were born, God has numbered our days: "Your eyes saw my unformed body; all the days ordained for me were written in your book before one of them came to be." This passage became an anchor for me as the years passed without my son Michael. I am not sure why God numbered his days as He did. I must trust that through it all, Michael completed his days. Down deep in my spirit, I am at peace, knowing Michael was able to accomplish his purpose in life.

My father once told me that sometimes God requires the very best. To this day I am not sure how he came to that conclusion. When my father was at a loss for words, he occasionally said unusual things. I was grateful for his attempt, but only God could speak in a way that could make me lie down in green pastures, lead me beside still waters, and restore my soul (Psalm 23:2-3a). In my heart I will always remember Michael with love and tenderness, and I have a special place in my soul reserved for my loving, sensitive son. I will always cherish his memory.

One of the most difficult questions a theologian has to answer is, "Why do bad things happen to good people?" Or conversely, "Why do good things happen to bad people?" Every day, we ask why certain events take place—events that do not seem fair or equitable from our point of view. An innocent child is born with a birth defect or a disability, and we ask, "Why?" A drunk driver causes an accident, killing another driver, and we ask, "Why did God allow this to happen to an innocent person?" Every day, we see examples of the inhumanity of mankind and attempt to blame God as if He had some culpability in our actions.

Our world suffers as a result of the free will of mankind. The freedom of choice was given to Adam and Eve in the Garden of Eden. Initially, our freedom was meant to be a blessing; however, disobedience ensued as the first humans departed from God's will. Now, mankind lives in a fallen world, shaped by our choices. In this world, bad things can happen as the result of generations of free will.

Free will from the perspective of heaven is unique to mankind. Neither angels nor demons possess the autonomy free will has to offer. Too often, innocent people find themselves brutalized by the free will of others. It is thought that, because we serve a God who created all things and knows all things, He should use His autonomy to make change. When God is silent, we think He doesn't care. Every night on the news, we witness firsthand the wickedness of mankind, as we hear reports of murder and mayhem. People wonder why God does not put an end to these injustices. Perhaps God has abandoned us.

When David was in the hospital, it was easy for me to think I had lost favor with God. The timing and severity of the event was too coincidental to ignore. God must be punishing me for some reason. When I look back at my life, I can think of countless reasons for God to be angry at my actions. David had lived a rather innocent life. It strikes me as unfath- 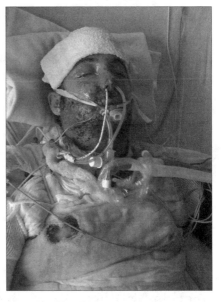 omable that God would inflict this illness on him in an effort to gain my attention. David is respectful, kind, loving, compassionate, and caring. He loves church and listens to Christian music all the time. He avoids trouble and tries each day to overcome the effects of autism.

Why, God? Why is David the one to suffer? Why not somebody else? Surely there must be thousands of individuals more deserving of this type of suffering. Perhaps a murderer or rapist would be a better choice. But the truth is, I am not God. Neither can I second-guess His wisdom. I knew I was in the midst of a twisted testimony I desperately wanted to avoid.

In the verse at the beginning of this chapter, Jesus and the disciples encountered a blind man. The disciples were trying to make sense of the man's disability. They thought there was a sinister reason for his blindness. Then Jesus said something unexpected. Rather than assigning blame to some supposed sin, He talked about the ability of the blind man to bring glory to God through his blindness: that the works of God might be displayed in him. According to Jesus, sin was not the reason for blindness in this man.

I would venture to say the parents of this man blamed themselves throughout their lifetime, thinking some sin they'd committed had led to their son's blindness. Perhaps they could remember a time when they purposefully broke a commandment of God. These moments of weakness when they lied, stole, or cursed God lay in the back of their minds as they tried to attach meaning to the event.

I believe we all tend to have similar thoughts when disaster strikes. But this blame game destroys families and relationships, all because we assume someone must be responsible for angering God. The story of the blind man should make us more sensitive to individuals going through trials.

My heart goes out to people who struggle every day, caring for a disabled loved one who cannot properly take care of their own needs. Families with special-needs children are especially vulnerable to regret as the mind attempts to reconcile the disability through blame. A common belief is that God is punishing them for some reason. Unfortunately, well-intentioned people can be cruel as they mimic the views of the disciples 2000 years ago. God has formed each of us. Psalm 139:13-15 says, "For you created my inmost being; you knit me together in my mother's womb. I praise you because I am fearfully and wonderfully made; your works are wonderful, I know that full well. My frame was not hidden from you when I was made in the secret place, when I was woven together in the depths of the earth."

The question still remains: Why me? Why my child? There are no good answers to the questions on this side of heaven. Perhaps we need to consider our world. We live in a fallen world and therefore everyone has a disability of some kind. The spectrum of human ability ranges from those who have great skill to those who have little or no physical or emotional ability. Our mindset should be one of compassion as we help the less fortunate find fulfillment.

When I was young, my father talked about his days in the military. He did not like to dwell on the war; however, he did from time to time talk about his experience as a tank gunner in World War II. His war experience was shockingly emotional. It left him with memories that tormented him for years.

My father fought as a member of a tank crew in a 200-plus tank division in the Battle of the Bulge in World War II. At the end of the battle, only three tanks remained from his division, and he was in one of them. He always wondered why he was spared. He asked the question in such a way that

I now know he suffered from survivor's guilt.

Besides that event, my father had another troubling experience later in the war. One afternoon, his tank came under fire and was pierced by a shell, killing everyone in his crew except him. In the blink of an eye, this shell bounced around inside the tank, slaughtering his friends while missing him completely. The unanswerable question of Why me? plagued him for years.

The question of "why" took on a different dimension for me one summer's day at my father's house shortly after his eighty-first birthday. I was sitting in his living room with him, talking about some of the ironies of life. He was proud of me and liked to show interest in my vocation by asking what seemed to be profound spiritual questions. On this occasion, he mentioned that he had outlived all his friends, and he wondered why. He continued by telling me that each year he received news about a relative or work acquaintance who had died.

It appeared to me my father still suffered from survivor's guilt. He looked at me and said, "If you had told me thirty years ago that I would live more than eighty years, outliving my friends, I would have laughed in your face." Then he asked me a strange question. "Son, why am I still alive?"

This caught me off guard. People usually asked me questions dealing with the negative, like why bad things happen to good people or why God took a loved one. I did not know how to respond to his question. Then he said, "I don't expect an answer from you."

After leaving my father's house that evening, I thought about his question. It seemed simple enough. Over the next few months, he experienced some health issues and was eventually hospitalized the following spring. While I visited him in the hospital, he again asked me the same question, "Son, why am I still alive?" Believing I did not have an answer, he deferred to the unknown mysteries of God.

He was surprised to learn that this time I had an answer. I told him I had thought about the response to this seemingly unanswerable question for quite some time, and I did, indeed, have an answer for him. His eyes lit up. "Tell me then. Why am I still alive?"

I said, "You're alive for the same reason I'm alive and everyone else is alive. Simply stated, we are alive because God said so. Without His permission, we cannot live. He has numbered our days and each of us lives with the same truth. A day is coming when God will no longer say so, and you will die."

Immediately, I detected relief on my father's face. His survival guilt dissipated when he was enlightened with this idea. Two months later, God stopped saying so, and my father was called to heaven.

~ 11 ~

In the Flame

Yet you, Lord, are our Father. We are the clay, you are the potter; we are all the work of your hand (Isaiah 64:8).

In the book of Jeremiah, God takes the prophet Jeremiah to the potter's house to teach him a great truth. God uses the art of pottery to describe how He shapes and fashions the world. As the potter has authority over the clay, God also has authority over us. All our trials and tribulations will somehow be of value as our "potter" shapes and molds us with His eternal means. As a potter with his clay, the Master spins the wheel of our life, forming us for His purpose. If the wheel damages or mars the clay, the potter has the ability to reshape the clay into a different vessel. When the clay has taken its final form, the potter places it into a fiery kiln to harden the object into a vessel of purpose. While the fire is intense, the vessel is placed there, because it has value to the potter.

Was God reshaping me through the fire of my circumstances? If so, what would the new vessel look like? Hospitals are often fiery kilns for people in distress. For me, the Survival Flight helicopter functioned as the kiln by which my faith and reliance upon God would be abundantly tested. Each day at the hospital, I felt the physical and emotional discomfort as the Potter rotated the wheel in an effort to shape me. The kiln, however, was unimaginable. The intensity of the furnace overwhelmed my spirit. I could only hope the intense fire would accelerate the drying process, which would bring about the vessel God intended. I began to think that, if I emerged as anything at all, it was only because the Potter determined it to be so. I had traveled this forsaken road before and felt absolutely alone.

The intense heat from the Potter's kiln radiated exactly ten years to the day of my first son's death. On this occasion, the fire's fury was directed toward David, and the prognosis was grim at best. As I considered the irony of this horrible circumstance, a Psalm, which had once given me peace, was brought to my remembrance. I thought, "Is Psalm 139:16 here again? Is this the day God ordained for David to die?" I struggled with the concept. The tombstone from Michael's gravesite flashed in my mind, as the embers of death were present.

While we were in the waiting room, I remember telling my wife that Psalm 139 is as true on the bad days as it is on the good days. If this was the day God had numbered for David to die, then I would have to be good with it. But if this was not the day God had numbered for David, then he would live and not die. Either way, we had nothing to worry about. He was in God's hands.

My wife's favorite verse is Romans 8:28: "And we know that in all things God works for the good of those who love him, who have been called according to his purpose." She believed God would somehow reveal to us a greater purpose in this suffering, even though she was bewildered by our circumstances. It did not appear to me that God was working any good on my behalf; therefore, I had to conclude that I didn't love Him the way He wanted me to. This verse added stress to me as I thought about the ramifications of no hope.

Over and over again, she cited Romans 8, much like I cited Psalm 139. Romans 8 is an active Scripture, telling us what is going to happen. Psalm 139, on the other hand, is more passive, acknowledging and resting in the unknowable sovereignty of God. Her strength came from the promises contained within Romans 8, whereas I was more comfortable acquiescing to Psalm 139.

I have often struggled with Romans 8, because suffering tends to blind those going through adversity. I was in the midst of emotional pain; I did not think the crisis could provide a positive purpose. From my vantage point, pain and sadness proceeded in every direction. David had already endured many obstacles in life, dealing with autism, Michael's death, depression, poor self-image, and a pessimistic view of the world. It was nearly impossible to see how adding a life-threatening illness could ever have a positive effect on anyone's life. I simply could not accommodate the truth in Romans 8 as I watched my son suffer.

I knew David's life was in God's hands. This burden of regret, anger, and hopelessness lifted as I reflected on the truth that God is in control. Immediately, I realized that every minute of every day has been ordained in some fashion by God. It is He who defines every breath, every thought, and every moment of our day.

~ 12 ~

The Challenge to Trust

I know that my redeemer lives, and that in the end he will stand on the earth. And after my skin has been destroyed, yet in my flesh I will see God (Job 19:25-26).

With all the problems we were juggling every day, my thoughts turned to a biblical character who is the epitome of suffering. The story of Job is found in the Old Testament Scriptures and is believed to be one of the oldest writings of the Hebrew Bible. The story begins much like a modern-day novel, as we are introduced to the primary characters.

In the land of Uz there lived a man whose name was Job. This man was blameless and upright; he feared God and shunned evil. He had seven sons and three daughters, and he owned seven thousand sheep, three thousand camels, five hundred yoke of oxen and five hundred donkeys, and had a large number of servants. He was the greatest man among all the people of the East (Job 1:1-3).

Job was rich by the standards of the day, with the blessing of family, friends, and influence. Oddly enough, his fortunes are not the reason for his inclusion in the Holy Scriptures. We learn about this incredible man because of his reaction to extreme suffering. As the story develops, the reader is told that Job was pleasing to God and honored God in every way.

Job's story is not an account filled with pleasant experiences. Unknown to Job, he was being used as a human pawn in a battle between God and Satan. While the book of Job has multiple themes, the absolute sovereignty of God is the focus throughout the narrative. Satan appears to have access to the councils of God and is able to enter into God's presence to communicate with Him. Satan has gone throughout the world, wondering if mankind was truly devoted and genuine in their worship of God.

> *The Lord said to Satan, "Have you considered my servant Job? There is no one on earth like him; he is blameless and upright, a man who fears God and shuns evil. Does Job fear God for nothing?" Satan replied. "Have you not put a hedge around him and his household and everything he has? You have blessed the work of his hands, so that his flocks and herds are spread throughout the land. But now stretch out your hand and strike everything he has, and he will surely curse you to your face"* (Job 1:8-11).

The stage had been set for an unusual test. According to God, Job was unlike any person alive on the earth. He served God faithfully and without reservation. Satan believed Job's devotion was based entirely on God's blessing. In fact, Satan appears to be complaining about the favored status God gave Job. He believed if God removed the many blessings, Job would curse Him to His face.

God, who searches the heart and minds of everyone, has a distinct advantage over Satan as He proclaims the loyalty and tenacity of His servant. As the drama unfolds, the tapestry of Job's life unravels in a way that strikes terror into the hearts of people who view God as always fair and just. Satan was allowed to take Job's wealth, the lives of his family, and his health. Through no fault of his own, he suffered at the hand of Satan as he lived out a faithful life to God.

I remember thinking about this story as I went through emotional agony at the hospital. The stress of the situation was becoming more than I could bear. Although I am not like Job at all, I was beginning to think the gap between my pain and his suffering was narrowing quickly. My world was falling apart and the attacks against my family were taking their toll on me. Like Job, I felt overpowered or abandoned by God. I wondered if He cared about my troubles.

Job must have felt like an innocent bystander as these events took place. Outwardly, he appeared to be cursed beyond all measure. He was not a lukewarm worshipper of God. One would think God would surely bless him for his loyalty and worship. In fact, he should be a prime candidate for perpetual health, wealth, and happiness.

Job's devotion in obeying God far exceeded any attempts in my life to follow Him. Events were happening beyond my control, but they were also beyond belief. I wondered who was attacking me—Satan or God. I hoped Satan was responsible for the attacks, because God could limit Satan on my behalf. I'd rather have Satan mad at me than to have God angry with me. Where could I turn if God was angry?

I can imagine Job struggling in his relationship with God while facing one trial after another. It must have been difficult for him to see his circumstances as anything but a curse. I think it is natural to view good things as well as bad things within the light of blessings and curses. It is obvious that Job played no part in his misfortunes. His friends tried to reason with him, using the blame game. His close friends suggested he was at fault. His first friend said,

Consider now: Who, being innocent, has ever perished? Where were the upright ever destroyed? As I have observed, those who plow evil and those who sow trouble reap it (Job 4:7-8).

His second friend continued with the character assassination:

Surely God does not reject one who is blameless or strengthen the hands of evildoers (Job 8:20).

His third friend added,

If you put away the sin that is in your hand and allow no evil to dwell in your tent, then, free of fault, you will lift up your face; you will stand firm and without fear (Job 11:14-15).

The advice from his three friends continues with almost endless accusations against their friend. Finally, his wife added the coup de grace (final blow) to Job by encouraging him to curse God and die (Job 2:9).

Ultimately, Job was given a second chance at life and family. He fathered more children and enjoyed his new family as he watched a new generation born as a result of God's blessing. The personal cost to Job was still incredibly high. His new family would bring joy, gratitude, and love, but at the same time, the grave markers of his first children would be a constant reminder of the price paid in heaven as God and Satan battled over his character.

The New Testament describes Satan as a prowling and

roaring lion, walking the earth and seeking someone to devour. One of his intended targets was Simon Peter. In the Gospel of Luke, Jesus says,

Simon, Simon, Satan has asked to sift all of you as wheat. But I have prayed for you, Simon, that your faith may not fail. And when you have turned back, strengthen your brothers (Luke 22:31).

Many times, I felt as if I were in a lion's den, waiting to be the next dinner.

The Bible gives us a roadmap to help us avoid the heartaches our world tries to inflict upon us. In the books of Psalms and Proverbs, David and Solomon give us inspirational wisdom. Proverbs contain many if /then statements. If you do this, then this is sure to happen. Most of the time, certain outcomes will be the result as people apply these principles to their life. For example, Proverbs 22:6 says,

Start children off on the way they should go, and even when they are old they will not turn from it.

The thought is that if you give children the proper foundation, they are much more likely to make the right choices when they are older. If they do not have this instruction, they will not have a support system from which to draw solid solutions when they get older. This does not mean children cannot reject the fundamental teaching they received and choose instead to act on their free will. Rather, it is more likely that they will do what they have been taught.

What would you do if God removed your blessings? Would you curse Him to His face? Would you complain about fairness? What would you say to God if you lost your family, wealth, and health? How would you feel if you discovered it was all part of a master plan because you loved God? This idea once again filled my mind as fairness and providence entered my thoughts.

Have I ever felt like Job? I can't say I understand his suffering. He was an incredible man of God, who suffered as a result of Satan's attack. Although my circumstances seemed unfair, I could only hope God would someday use my testimony to touch the hearts of people in crisis.

Have you considered my servant Job? There is no one on earth like him; he is blameless and upright, a man who fears God and shuns evil (Job 1:8).

~ 13 ~

Raging Storms

If I say, "Surely the darkness will hide me and the light become night around me," even the darkness will not be dark to you; the night will shine like the day, for darkness is as light to you (Psalm 139:1-2).

David clung to life by a thread when a social worker talked to me about bringing his brother Stephen to see him. She did not believe David would recover and thought I needed to give Stephen the opportunity to say goodbye. I had to fight every pessimistic thought that suggested I should yield to the situation and give up on David and his struggle to live. She suggested that, in the absence of information, Stephen might make up a scenario that would frighten him in a way that was worse than the actual events. I could not honestly conceive of a worse scenario than the truth. The chance of Stephen's imagination conceiving something more frightening was remote.

I was not prepared to say goodbye to David, so why should I ask Stephen to? The suggestion alerted me to use caution as my paternal instincts kicked in. I went to great lengths to shelter Stephen from the graphic details of the events surrounding David's ordeal. I was as optimistic as I could be and demonstrated a great deal of faith as I talked to

Stephen. I did not want him to see his brother suffering in this state. David was semi-conscious, on a ventilator, and looked like a mummy in his head-to-toe bandages. At this stage, chances were good that Stephen would not have recognized him anyway.

My faith was being tested at every juncture. I never doubted God or His ability to heal. Rather, I was not sure if He planned to intervene in this illness and give David a second chance. Faith is described in the Bible as the substance of things hoped for, the evidence of things not seen (Hebrews 11:1). It is clear by this statement that I needed hope when hope was fading. Even the smallest amount of faith has substance. I remembered this saying of Jesus:

> *Truly I tell you, if you have faith as small as a mustard seed, you can say to this mountain, "Move from here to there,"' and it will move. Nothing will be impossible for you* (Matthew 17:20).

Each day, disaster stalked me at every turn, and the light of hope only reflected its shadow. With hope fading, my faith was tested under the stress. I thought about faith and what it meant in this situation. There remained a dim, flickering light of faith in the depths of my soul, which gave me hope in the desperate hours. I was looking for a way to strengthen the light of faith before it was extinguished. I prayed my faith would not fail and hoped it would make a difference in David's outcome.

There are times in my life when my surroundings were calm and stable. This was clearly not one of those times. I have learned how quickly events can change. In the blink of an eye, joy can turn to sorrow and sorrow can turn to joy. The

Bible describes how quickly circumstances can change. The disciples were traveling by boat across the Sea of Galilee when they encountered a dangerous storm. They believed they were in danger of drowning and cried out for Jesus to help them. The story is recorded in Matthew 8:23-27.

> *Then he got into the boat and his disciples followed him. Suddenly a furious storm came up on the lake, so that the waves swept over the boat. But Jesus was sleeping. The disciples went and woke him, saying, "Lord, save us! We're going to drown!" He replied, "You of little faith, why are you so afraid?" Then he got up and rebuked the winds and the waves, and it was completely calm. The men were amazed and asked, "What kind of man is this? Even the winds and the waves obey him!"*

How many times have we believed Jesus didn't care about our circumstances or thought He must be sleeping? How many times have we relied upon ourselves when we were in the midst of disaster? The phrase "We're in this boat together" takes on new meaning when we consider Jesus is in our boat. According to the biblical narrative, Jesus was sleeping on the boat as the waves and the storm tossed it about. The disciples feared they would perish at sea. In some respects, they must have wondered if the sleeping Jesus cared at all. Fear was so great in their hearts, they seemed to forget the Creator of the universe was on the boat!

The circumstances of the storm changed the paradigm of the fishermen. These men were familiar with storms. I would bet they thought they were in control of their situation. As the storm grew beyond the disciples' ability to cope, they awoke Jesus for help. Within seconds after Jesus rebuked the wind and the waves, the sea was absolutely calm. Imagine for a moment the irony of the situation. Minutes earlier, the wind and waves pushed the boat at a rapid rate across the sea and in an instant the ship lay motionless. No longer fearing for their lives, they began rowing to the distant shore.

The disciples were in a boat with the Almighty. It does not matter how large or small your boat is if Jesus is on the journey with you. If you are going through pain and suffering, consider for a moment that Jesus is in the boat. When you're sick, Jesus is in the boat. When financial disaster strikes, Jesus is in the boat. Finally, as death approaches, Jesus is in the boat with you. He alone can calm the seas and direct the path of the wind.

~ 14 ~

David's Near-Death Experiences

For I am convinced that neither death nor life, neither angels nor demons, neither the present nor the future, nor any powers, neither height nor depth, nor anything else in all creation, will be able to separate us from the love of God that is in Christ Jesus our Lord (Romans 8:38-39).

For two and a half weeks, David remained in U of M's burn trauma ICU. Every moment of every day, we wondered if he would live to see another day, another hour, or another minute. Most of the time, we wondered if he would see another minute.

As the storms of death crashed against our shores, I wondered if Jesus was in the boat with us. I felt as if I had been bailing the water of dismal news for days, and I was exhausted. My mind was tormented and tired. I was becoming accustomed to disappointment. Unbeknownst to me, as David lay motionless, God was revealing dreams and visions to him. David was in a place where only God could speak to him.

David's near-death experience was the first installment in a series of angelic encounters and dreams. David recounted two separate angelic encounters and an out-of-body experience while he was in the hospital. The following is the se-

77

quence of events in chronological order of the near-death experience David had while he was in the ICU. Perhaps you too can find comfort in David's story as you read the account of angels and heaven.

In the quiet place between life and death, David experienced the light of God as death knocked at his door. He ascended into a tunnel of light, where his autism could no longer follow him. For the first time in his life, he experienced profound clarity of thought that allowed him to understand a greater reality. God had sent angels to comfort him and a Lamb to heal him.

David's first experience began with simple and common things in his hospital room. He saw familiar images that were part of his surroundings. He saw a helicopter fly by as the early morning sun began to rise. Standing at David's window, we could see the hospital's heliport; however, if we were near his bed, the heliport was out of sight. David would have had to look through the solid wall behind his headboard to see the heliport.

His first experience included an out-of-body awareness, in which he floated above his body. He looked out the window, and the sun appeared exceedingly bright in comparison to the earth below, which was dark. The room was also dark. As he turned from side to side in his vantage point above, he could see people working on him as he lay in his bed. He saw a light similar to a candle coming from each person in the room. He looked around the room and, to his amazement, the objects lit as if his eyes were functioning as a flashlight.

Above him, a greater light appeared, shining with the brightness of the sun. The light was soft yet brilliantly beautiful. It had appeared from above him in the shape of a tunnel. He felt himself drawn to it, much like a moth to a flame. He began to ascend as the light shone on him. When the light completely encircled him, David heard the voices of people who were praying for him. The prayers were gathered up into the light, much like sound waves traveling to a specific destination. They ascended with David and he could hear bits and pieces of the prayers. Soon, a chorus of prayers, which were being said on his behalf, encompassed him. He was caught up in the light, as were the prayers. It was as if the prayers that surrounded him had a purpose as they travelled toward the light.

The countless prayers and voices were indistinguishable to David. This experience reminded him of being in a large room full of people talking to one another. As you walk through the room, the overall noise levels are loud enough to keep you from hearing the individual conversations. However, as you walk through the room, you can hear bits and pieces of conversations close to you. As you continue to walk through the room, those conversations fade and other conversations, which could not be heard earlier, can now be heard. In a similar fashion, the prayers in the vortex of light could not be isolated long enough for him to understand them individually.

David remembers being surprised when his autism no longer impeded his ability to understand his surroundings. Normally, David was horrified to be in a situation with many voices and background noise. In this place, the voices, noise, and uncertainty did not cause confusion or anxiety, nor did they diminish his ability to appreciate his surroundings. David describes this feeling as his "head being clear." Autism was no longer a problem, as he was totally free from its influence.

While David was ascending into the light, he listened intently to the voices and prayers. His ascent stopped when he focused on specific voices while trying to comprehend what was spoken. He knew the prayers were about him. Soon the prayers decreased in number and the voices could be distinguished as those of his family. The last voice praying was singular, and female. While the voice was familiar, David was not sure to whom it belonged. He thought it might have been an aunt or someone over the age of forty. He remembered one prayer: "God, please don't let David die." After this last voice faded, David looked toward the earth below and knew he must go back to his life. At this point, he believed that he had died. As he told me about his experience, I remembered my wife telling me that she had repeatedly prayed that exact prayer when he was in critical condition.

David's next memory was of a beautiful garden. He was lying on the ground, and standing around him were four angels. These messengers stared at him; however, they did not speak. He sat up and spent a few moments looking from side to side. This garden place had brilliant green, knee-high grass and large rolling hills that extended well beyond his understanding of the horizon. The terrain appeared to extend forever in every direction. To David, heaven appeared flat, without the curvature of the earth.

In every direction, the light from this place was beautiful and magnificent. An enormous tree with a large trunk and low branches stood majestically on a small mound a few hundred yards from him. The trunk was larger in diameter than any tree known on earth. Its massive branches extended in every direction, even reaching toward the ground like giant tentacles. The tree was full, shaped like a half-circle, and beautifully lit.

While David was in the garden, he felt like a beautiful child of God. David also remembers seeing a large pair of hands. In these large hands was a lamb, and the lamb was placed on his lap. David said, "Father, why is the lamb on my lap?" A voice, which he assumed was God's, told him the lamb was going to heal him.

When I asked David why he thought the voice was God's, he replied that he used the word "Father" instinctively. He did not even think to address the one with the lamb in his hands as anyone other than "Father."

After the voice told David the lamb was going to heal him, he was overcome with peace and love, because he knew God was communicating with him. He also knew he would return to his body and to his life.

Initially, David was disappointed at the thought of leaving this place of peace and serenity to return to a body full of pain and suffering. Additionally, any fear of death he once had was completely gone. In this garden was unspeakable joy. He had experienced breathtaking moments in the presence of angels; he was free from autism, and it felt wonderful.

David remembers returning to his body and having trouble breathing. He thought for a moment that he was still dying. He called out to God and said, "God, You said the lamb was going to heal me. Why am I still dying?" Immediately, he could breathe again. He felt God had just breathed into him the breath of life once again.

The concept of time meant little to David as he rested in

his room. He was not aware of its passage at all. For a brief moment in his experience, eternity intersected with the natural world, making time irrelevant. As the New Testament states in 2 Peter 3:8, with the Lord a day is like a thousand years, and a thousand years are like a day. David did not know if hours or days had passed before his next encounter took place.

In this dream, David was in the presence of two angels. He noticed he had a helmet on his head. He did not like the helmet and wanted very much to remove it. One of the angels, who called him by his name, told him that if he removed the helmet, he would die. David understood the helmet was a reference to his body. By removing his helmet (body), he would enter death. The angels looked much like human beings; however, they had a countenance about them that was quite different. While they did have arms and legs and bodies, David instinctively understood they were angels. When I asked him how he knew, in his innocence he replied, "You just know."

The second angelic encounter was also in the form of a dream. This dream began in an unusual setting. David was a crewmember on a balloon-shaped ship. There were many people on this ship with him. Some people were happy, while others were sad. The sad ones did not know where they were going. He did not know any of them. He was part of the crew and was suffering from an injury that would lead to his death.

The angel spoke to him and said, "David, don't give up. You have the power to get through it." In that moment, David believed the only reason he survived was because the angel encouraged him to fight for his life.

I have often wondered about the meaning in this remarkable experience. Were these unknown people on their way to heaven? Did they die unexpectedly? Why were some happy and some sad? I wish I had the answer to these questions. Nevertheless, God has given David an insight that others seldom experience.

David was experiencing a remarkable place full of love, encouragement, and peace. His view was much greater than mine as the peace of heaven overcame the storms of chaos that plagued him. God was revealing great things to him. God was in the background, calming the storms for David.

Jesus had not left him adrift on the boat alone. While it is true that many obstacles still lay in his path, he now had the light of hope from God, which illuminated his path and pierced the darkness.

David's near-death experience gave him a second chance to see himself from the perspective of heaven. He now understands that God views him as His child and therefore a beautiful person. This experience has greatly diminished the effects of autism in his life. While it is true that he is still autistic with Asperger's, the sting of autism (so to speak) has been removed and replaced by a greater view. He has a view of himself from the perspective of an eternal garden. If we all could see ourselves from this perspective, just imagine what the effect would be in our lives.

~ 15 ~

The Whisper of Eternity

*Show me, Lord, my life's end and the number of my days;
let me know how fleeting my life is. You have made my
days a mere handbreadth; the span of my years is as
nothing before you. Everyone is but a breath, even those
who seem secure. Surely everyone goes around like a mere
phantom; in vain they rush about, heaping up wealth
without knowing whose it will finally be* (Psalm 39:4-6).

Perspective is an amazing thing. It shapes the way we
view our circumstances. Our lives are but a vapor against the
backdrop of eternity. We spend every moment in this life at-
tempting to secure our future on earth and miss the greater
view of eternity. The truth is that we cannot have lasting security on earth. We do not know what tomorrow holds for us;
neither do we know how long we or anyone else will live.
Only God has the answers to life and death. In Matthew
6:34, Jesus tells us not to worry about tomorrow, for tomorrow will worry about itself. Each day has enough trouble
of its own.

Our only true security is in eternity. Heaven is our abode
if we are in Christ. He controls heaven as well as the earth.
Therefore, whether we live or die, we do so according to
God's purpose. Simply stated, God is in control. In our so-

ciety of freedom and self-determination, it is not popular to acknowledge that everything we have comes from the gracious hand of God. God's grace in my circumstances meant breath to David and everything to me. Daily I clung to my faith, but my perspective was still based on what my eyes could see and my mind could accept. I could only hope David would recover, but his illness painted a bleak picture in my mind. In the clouded mist of trials, my focus remained on what I could see and the desperation of the situation.

David, on the other hand, had a completely different perspective. He was given a glimpse of a heavenly realm for a brief moment. He felt unconditional love and intense joy. The physical and emotional issues that had plagued him his entire life had disappeared. He innately knew he had to return to his body, but he longed to stay in that place forever.

From the dawn of time, mankind has had a profound fascination with death and the afterlife. The concept of death strikes unbelievable fear into the human heart. It is a ceaseless enemy that relentlessly pursues all people until the abyss of death encompasses them. Death respects no one, stealing joy, hope, encouragement, and peace. Death is in opposition to life, never giving hope to anyone. It is a one-way door to the grave, keeping all who enter. Try as you may, you cannot escape the grasp of death when it finally arrives.

When my son Michael died, the hopelessness of death tormented me. I was devastated and felt as if my spirit had been crushed. Each day, I tried to reconcile the loss as I thought about him. The loss, grief, and anger overwhelmed me at times, and my heart suffered from a lack of appreciation for anything. I was one parent among many who had suffered the loss of a child.

Death is the absence of everything. David's near-death experience had delivered him to the portals of death as it sought to strip him of everything. His angelic encounters mitigated death as his spirit entered into the presence of God. David no longer fears death because death cannot steal his spirit. God has shown him marvelous blessings within the light of His kingdom.

David's near-death experience has been a blessing to me as I struggle with the emotions associated with Michael's death. Through David's experience, God has removed the shroud of death in my heart by giving David a second chance at life. My crushed spirit began to soar as He redeemed all the pain that death had previously inflicted.

For our light and momentary troubles are achieving for us an eternal glory that far outweighs them all. So we fix our eyes not on what is seen, but on what is unseen, since what is seen is temporary, but what is unseen is eternal (2 Corinthians 4:17-18).

Our time on this earth is temporary and finite. It begins with our birth and ends with our death. The trials we face in life are also temporary and finite when compared to eternity.

The Holy Bible gives us great insights into life, death, heaven, hell, and the afterlife. The Hebrew Scriptures describe death as a state in which we no longer experience love, joy, wealth, suffering, pain, or any other emotion. Our physical body, which once had the breath of life from God, is now an empty shell without influence or power. Our material bodies eventually return to dust as the physical portion of our existence ends. The spiritual aspect is all that remains of the human soul after death.

Our life on earth is the culmination of the physical being as well as the spiritual being. We hear a lot about the differences between body, soul, and spirit, and yet they are connected. What is the body without the soul or the soul without the spirit? As human beings, we have a material physical part (body) as well as an immaterial part (soul/spirit).

I believe that, at the instant of death, our material part is permanently separated from the immaterial portion. This body-soul combination is now completely dead without any ability to communicate with the living, because death has severed them. The spirit portion (which came to us as the breath of God giving us life) is returned to its Creator in heaven. For we must all appear before the judgment seat of Christ, so that each of us may receive what is due us for the things done while in the body, whether good or bad (2 Corinthians 5:10). The apostle Paul's statements were directed to people who had received Christ by faith. Therefore, we can conclude that redeemed people will be present with the Lord in some fashion after they die.

The afterlife is a place where time has no meaning. God is from everlasting to everlasting. Time was created by God and has a specific purpose. In Genesis chapter 1, God introduces the concept of evening and morning and how they combine to make a day. These ideas of time continued until the fourth day, when God started a galactic time clock by the creation of the stars, planets, and universe. This evening and morning concept does not exist in heaven as it does on earth. Our heavenly state is a place where God is and where time has no meaning.

God's Word gives us comfort when everything around us

is falling apart, softening all the pain and heartache of unbelievable loss. How many times have we heard that in heaven, God will wipe every tear from our eyes, and there will be no more death or sorrow or crying or pain? All our suffering and injustices will be gone forever.

If you have experienced loss through the death of someone you love, know that God holds each person in eternity. They have not been lost nor forgotten. They reside in a place outside of time. This is why it's so important to respond to the gospel message. The circumstances of one's death are not nearly as important as the circumstances of one's life.

David was never declared clinically dead, even though he thought he was. His near-death experience was such a unique phenomenon, he reasoned he had entered death because his autism was gone, his pain was gone, angels were present, and God sent a lamb to heal him. I think that, given these circumstances, anyone would think they had died and gone to heaven.

I now can view death as a powerful spiritual occurrence. While death ends our physical existence, the spiritual component survives the trauma of death in eternity. In death, individuals are not capable of communicating with the living. The shroud of death has obscured all knowledge of the afterlife. Is there life after death? The Scriptures clearly report a spiritual realm as well as a resurrection. Heaven and hell are real, as are angels, demons, and God. Both heaven and hell are not as far away as one may think.

~ 16 ~

Heaven

My Father's house has many rooms; if that were not so, would I have told you that I am going there to prepare a place for you? And if I go and prepare a place for you, I will come back and take you to be with me that you also may be where I am (John 14:1-3).

When I think of heaven, thoughts of beauty, peace, love, joy, fulfillment, awe, everlasting life, and blessedness in the presence of God and His holy angels come to mind. It is hard for me to comprehend the nuances of each adjective because I have not experienced heaven from the perspective of a soul view. When David describes heaven, his thoughts and ideas have been turned into feelings, as each adjective radiates in full color in his spirit. His perspective is not from what his physical eye has seen or ear heard; rather, his soul underwent a spiritual metamorphosis as his body lay dormant in a darkened hospital room. His near-death experience has brought depth, height, and breath to his understanding of heaven.

In the quiet place between life and death, David experienced an amazing phenomenon and shares his story of encountering light, angels, and heaven while unconscious and clinging to life. Having one foot in the grave and the other in heaven, he stood at the edge of death. From this pedestal, the marvels of his near-death experience find meaning.

In the modern era, the death experience has taken on new meaning, as medical science has extended the ability of mankind to reclaim people from the precipice of death. Advances in medicine and medical techniques have redefined the limits of mortality. Patients no longer succumb to conditions that were once considered life-ending. With the recent increase in near-death experiences, our culture has gained unusual information never before available to mankind. This unique portal has fueled the imaginations of many and therefore should be put into proper perspective as the Word of God speaks to this generation.

Today, near-death experiences thrive in a technological age. However, independent near-death accounts cannot be validated in a scientific manner; neither can they be confirmed by a spiritual understanding, as they are subjective and open to interpretation. People from all over the world with different creeds and cultures are reporting comparable types of experiences, indicating that this unusual phenomenon is not exclusive to any specific religion or spirituality.

David's experience showed him a unique spiritual dimension that exists between life and death as the afterlife merges with the natural world. These experiences are, by definition, not death. Rather, they are accounts from people who believe they have died and have returned to life. While the body appears dead in a clinical sense, the breath of life remains in the body in some small way, providing a gateway back to conscious life.

Stories of angels and heaven are becoming commonplace in the literary world and on social media as books and the Internet connect a community of people who have had unexplained, profound near-death experiences. The religious community tends to be extremely cautious of claims made by people who report these events. Historically, claims of encountering angels and seeing the abode of heaven are rare events seen only in the pages of the Bible. Additionally, the Bible speaks of demons and hell and how redemption from these powers is crucial if heaven is the ultimate goal.

As a Christian, I believe in heaven and hell, angels, demons, and the afterlife. It is not the intent of this book to provide a view of heaven in opposition to the Holy Scriptures. Rather, the Bible provides the foundations of truth as we examine life, death, and eternity against the backdrop of modern day near-death experiences. Neither is it the intent of this book to provide definitive answers on the subject of these experiences. David's experience is a personal epiphany of profound joy within God's creation. He wants to share his experience with others who are willing to listen and can receive the message. The raging debate that centers on the authenticity of near-death experiences will no doubt continue for years to come.

There are skeptics who do not accept near-death experiences as credible. Some of these skeptics see only the natural world around them and view a near-death experience as lunacy, while others who believe in the supernatural may attribute these experiences to euphoria of some type. For the purposes of this discussion, I would like to place the skeptics into two major categories.

Several groups doubt the spiritual aspect of near-death experiences. The first major category includes people referred to as atheists. Atheists, as a general rule, do not believe in God, heaven, or the supernatural realm. Due in part to their belief, they lack the capacity to consider heaven, because they tend to see the universe from only a natural perspective. Scientific proof is the only measurement they consider when referring to unusual events. Any system with a spiritual aspect cannot be counted as credible to them. This group would view near-death experiences as the natural processes of the brain as it nears death. It is unlikely they could ever accept the possibility that near-death experiences have a spiritual component, because the spiritual realm does not exist to them.

The atheist believes the near-death experience is a special kind of euphoria experienced when the brain releases certain chemicals prior to death. Therefore, they think the experience is part imagination and part chemical stimulation.

The second major group of people is known as theists. Theists generally believe in the existence of God. They agree that God is responsible for everything; however, they disagree as to when and how He created everything. Theists believe in the spiritual realm as well as the afterlife. They generally have a belief system based on Scripture. Theists are divided on the authenticity of near-death experiences. Some believe they can occur and are from God, while others find these claims to be suspect.

Theologically, making a case for near-death experiences is difficult, due to the lack of scriptural references that address them. However, we can find biblical instances of people having dreams and visions, as well as seeing angels. The following list contains a few biblical examples of ordinary people having dreams or encountering angels.

- Abraham encountered both God and angels at his house.

- Abimelech was warned by God in a dream not to touch Abraham's wife, Sarah.

- Lot entertained angels in Sodom and Gomorrah.

- As a child, Samuel had dreams given by God.

- Joseph and Daniel had the God-given gift of interpreting dreams.

- David saw an angel standing between heaven and earth.

- The apostles Peter and John both had visions from God.

Throughout time, God has used dreams and visions to communicate His messages to His people. Some God-given dreams required an interpreter to convey an accurate meaning. Angelic visitations are also mentioned numerous times throughout the Scriptures. Angels are real!

Hebrews 13:2 states, "Do not forget to show hospitality to strangers, for by so doing some people have shown hospitality to angels without knowing it." Bible scholars can testify to the existence of angelic encounters mentioned throughout Scripture. Encountering angels or having visions in today's day and age should not be considered unbiblical, given the words delivered at Pentecost: "In the last days, God says, I will pour out my Spirit on all people. Your sons and daughters will prophesy, your young men will see visions, your old men will dream dreams" (Acts 2-17).

It is not uncommon in this modern age to hear Christian pastors, teachers, and televangelists reveal to their congregations how God has been personally communicating with them in some way. I confess I am sometimes amazed at the length of the conversations they have with God. One would think they are listening to His actual audible voice. God has and does give His servants a word to share. Sometimes they receive this communication in a spiritual or intellectual fashion, outside the confines of the written Word. This type of sharing does not seem strange or unusual to those within the Christian community. Maybe God has spoken to them, and maybe He has not. I cannot say for sure, as it is not my place to judge how people encounter God.

The Spirit of God gives us the ability to hear the still, small voice that provides a connection with Him. As we listen to this voice, God manifests Himself to us. When people say they are listening to God and hearing His voice, I generally do not think they are crazy. God is not obligated to tell me whether or not He has spoken to them. The real issue for me is whether the message violates the known Word of God. If it is consistent with His Word, I will think about it further. However, I still do not know if he/she has, in fact, heard from the Lord.

"For my thoughts are not your thoughts, neither are your ways my ways," declares the Lord (Isaiah 55:8).

Could God communicate with people by using a near-death experience? The following is a story told by the apostle Paul:

I know a man in Christ who fourteen years ago was caught up to the third heaven. Whether it was in the body or out of the body I do not know—God knows. And I know that this man—whether in the body or apart from the body I do not know, but God knows—was caught up to paradise and heard inexpressible things, things that no one is permitted to tell (2 Corinthians 12:2-4).

Did this man have a near-death experience? Was he in the body or out of the body? The Apostle Paul, writing under the inspiration of the Holy Spirit, did not seem to know, so how can we? Only God knows. Do people who have near-death experiences have them in the third heaven or any other heaven? I don't know; only God knows.

Near-death experiences are subjective in nature and cannot be validated or proven. In most cases, extreme trauma accompanies the experience, and the encoding/decoding process may suffer as a result. I believe God is speaking to the spirit portion of consciousness, while the natural body knows nothing.

The Holy Scriptures inform us that:

The person without the Spirit does not accept the things that come from the Spirit of God but considers them fool-ishness, and cannot understand them because they are dis-cerned only through the Spirit (1 Corinthians 2:14).

Also, in verse 9:

What no eye has seen, what no ear has heard, and what no human mind has conceived" the things God has prepared for those who love him—these are the things God has re-vealed to us by his Spirit.

The physical portion of man beings cannot comprehend spiritual matters. Neither does our literal eye see, nor literal ear hear the wonders that await us when we finally reach heaven.

There are good and valid reasons why some Christians are skeptical of many of today's near-death experience accounts. The most common objection stems from the lack of true faith exhibited by the recipient of the experience. Some individuals have claimed to visit heaven without having faith in God's redemptive plan for mankind. I absolutely believe heaven is the dwelling place for the elect believers in Christ, as hell is the abode for non-believers.

The Christian doctrine of election might bridge the gap as current non-believers encounter a glimpse of heaven. "The elect" is a phrase used by God to identify human beings whose names are written in the Lamb's Book of Life. On earth, individuals are recognized as part of God's elect only after being born again, which is necessary if we want to go to heaven. Prior to faith in Christ, non-believers are not counted among the elect. Earthly time has made it impossible for us to know here on earth the identity of the elect. But while we are limited in this knowledge, God is not. Therefore, a near-death experience of an unbeliever would not be out of character if he/she were part of God's elect. God knows the unbeliever will eventually experience the saving faith necessary to be considered one of His elect at some point in the future.

Since these experiences are beyond our ability to examine scientifically, some people dismiss them as fiction. After much research, I've noticed some common elements that emerge as the individual stories are told. There is a sense of tremendous spiritual awe as each person relives the experience in his or her mind. Additionally, the stories are conveyed in a soft-spoken manner, displaying humility about the event. Even though detractors abound, they calmly relate an unimaginable experience.

These encounters fundamentally alter their self-image. In most cases, people who have gone through this type of enlightenment display a greater appreciation for life as well as humility toward God. They realize that not everyone has this type of experience and are grateful to have been given a second chance to view life differently.

In most cases, the experiences fall into two camps. One is of light, while the other is of darkness. The first type involves a tunnel accompanied by a beautiful or glorious light. The majority of the recorded accounts of near-death experiences claim this type of vision. People who experience a tunnel filled with light usually possess a new outlook on life, since this was a positive experience. Truly for them, death and life have new meaning.

David shares the joy of experiencing an existence free from the emotional and psychological limitations caused by his autism. His view of heaven has given him incredible strength to begin the process of socialization and become a witness to God's greatness. His new strength has tremendously increased his faith in Jesus and in God. I cannot find any cause for concern, as his spiritual journey has been enhanced by his experience. His faith is stronger, his love is greater, and he encourages others as a role model for families with special-needs children. Sharing his near-death experience has connected him to people who suffer physically.

The second type of experience involves great darkness and is associated with fear, pain, and torment. Those who have encountered great darkness seek a spiritual awakening and usually alter their lives as a result. It appears that God can use near-death experiences, whether positive or negative, to bring about profound change in a person's life.

The question that is begging to be asked is: do these two different accounts show us the difference between heaven and hell? I think in a minimalistic way, they do represent these two alternatives. To those who've had a near-death experience, the afterlife is no longer a theoretical issue. Heaven is absolutely real to them. They tell their stories of angels and light as if they were there! They also understand that, for the most part, people will not believe them. This lack of affirmation of their experience does not inhibit them from giving their testimony.

What is heaven like? It is clear that the Bible is the only real and tangible authority on this subject. Jesus conveyed truth about the kingdom of heaven by using idioms and concepts that were familiar to the assembled crowds. In the gospel accounts, Jesus spoke about the kingdom of heaven and what it is like: a treasure hidden in a field, a net, a merchant ship, yeast, a mustard seed,  a man sowing good seed, a king settling accounts, etc. Jesus, who knew heaven inside and out, used earthly, tangible things to describe that which is intangible to us (heaven).

I believe God has a specific purpose in mind when people have near-death experiences. These experiences give them a "heaven is like . . ." glimpse, getting them up close and personal with the kingdom of heaven. I believe heaven is infinitely greater and more glorious than anyone could possibly comprehend during any near-death experience. However it is written:

What no eye has seen, what no ear has heard, and what no human mind has conceived" the things God has prepared for those who love him (1 Corinthians 2:9).

Finally, God's Word contains great mysteries that are hidden from mankind. People throughout the Bible have had visions and dreams. They have seen angels and at times encounter God. In fact, the book of Revelation is filled with angels, dreams, and visions of heaven. The apostle John, writing on the island of Patmos, had many visions. In one vision, he saw the Holy Temple in heaven, as well as the final judgment. The Bible affirms the grandeur of a place called heaven. Heaven is a real place, and angels are real beings.

~ 17 ~

The Living Water

Whoever believes in me, as Scripture has said, rivers of living water will flow from within them" (John 7:38).

While David was in the hospital in Ann Arbor, I stayed at a local hotel to be near him and to save myself the three-hour round-trip commute from our home. I arranged to take vacation time from my job and requested extra time to care for him. Early each morning, I visited the nurse's station to ask if there were changes or any additional updates to report on his condition from the previous evening.

One morning, after a bandage change, the nurses had gathered in the hallway outside David's room, talking amongst themselves about a new development in his condition. I listened to their conversation as his mother and I walked toward his room. The nurses responsible for David's care that day said to one another, "Can you believe it? He has all his skin!"

My entire attitude changed from *Oh, God, I can't handle any more* to *Oh, God, tell me more.* I was focused and alert as the ramifications of new skin played out in my mind. The huge hurdle of having his body unprotected and vulnerable due to a lack of skin was finally over!

When Anna and I looked into the room, we could see

that David's body was no longer heavily bandaged. For the first time in two and a half weeks, we saw skin protecting his body. We knew the most critical obstacle in his path had been crushed. His new skin gave us fresh hope for a full recovery. I knew God's healing hand was upon him.

I talked to the nurses, soaking in every detail of what they had witnessed as they removed David's bandages earlier that morning. They said his new skin looked great and completely covered his entire body. They were surprised that his skin regenerated so quickly.

I immediately understood that David was finally emerging from this nightmare. I could see living waters of blessing. The tapestry of God included a mosaic of answered prayer. Looking at the bigger picture, it was not hard for me to believe God had been working in the background, healing my son. I told the nurses I could easily believe his exterior skin had regenerated so quickly because thousands of people had been praying for him.

I called my wife Renee, who was en route to her job. While we were talking, we both instinctively knew that an undeniable miracle had taken place. After work, she rushed to the hospital to see this miracle and celebrate with me. For the first time in weeks, I had a huge smile on my face and thankfulness in my heart. The stress and burden of David living on the edge had faded, and the dawn of a new day flourished around us.

The doctors were also extremely pleased to learn David had new skin covering his body. The good news continued when, later that day, they took him off the ventilator, and he began to breathe on his own. For the first time in what now seemed an eternity, I heard his sweet voice once again.

His voice was weak and soft as he tried to speak for the first time in weeks. Every sound was music to my ears as my son spoke hope back into my soul. The tones of his voice were once again familiar to me as the awesome breath of life proceeded from his lungs. For an instant, my mind flashed back to his birth, when I waited for a cry, a cough, or a sigh. I stood in an ocean of gratefulness as I listened to his faint words.

I spoke softly as I brought David up to date on his condition. I gave him what I call the optimistic *Reader's Digest* version of the past two and a half weeks. I told him the reason he could not see clearly was because he had membranes on his eyes to keep the scar tissue under his eyelids from scratching his cornea. I did not want him to think he was permanently blind as a result of SJS TEN. He did not say much; he was exhausted and needed to rest.

The news of his regenerated skin spread like wildfire as I placed calls to family and those who had been praying for him. In an instant, when I heard the word "recovery," the world had become a brighter place. I began to see the end of this nightmare.

The God who gives second chances had given David a second chance at life. It was exciting to see Him remove some of the final obstacles to my son's recovery. We were ecstatic to be in this moment, but at the same time, we wondered why God allowed him to beat the odds. "Why him?" The only thing I could think of was that God is good all the time, and all the time, God is good.

Soon, Anna and I were able to take David on short field trips to other parts of the hospital. I had been looking forward to this for a long time. I didn't know much about the hospital, but I was determined to find a peaceful place where David could feel the beauty of nature. I finally found a beautiful arboretum in the cardiac wing at the far end of the hospital. Anna wrapped several blankets around David to keep him warm on the excursion. We traveled the corridors with many people looking on.

We were excited to break free from the intensive care unit, if only for a short period. I couldn't stop smiling as we journeyed. David looked a little rough around the edges, but that did not deter us at all. We were overwhelmed with the joy of the moment. The travel time was about twenty minutes from the burn trauma unit to the cardiac unit by wheelchair. I was anxious to see what awaited us in the arboretum.

We reached our destination and it was beautiful indeed. It was a garden area, semi-enclosed by a glass exterior wall. This glass wall towered forty feet high, giving room for tall trees to grow. We also saw a beautiful stone waterfall that provided a rush of water to soothe our minds and bodies.

The scent of the arboretum was like a greenhouse after a summer rain. David couldn't see much of anything because of the membranes sewn on his eyes. But he could hear the rushing water and smell the vapors of life all around him. We sat there for what seemed hours, listening and enjoying the subtleties of peace. The waterfall amongst the rocks was steady and purposeful. This arboretum may not have been the Garden of Eden, but it was clearly the next best thing.

In the next week, we visited that arboretum every chance we could. David enjoyed the simple things as he sat listening to the sounds of water. This slice of paradise would be forever etched in our minds as we remember the feeling of hope in our small utopia.

~ 18 ~

The Love of a Brother

And now these three remain: faith, hope and love. But the greatest of these is love (1 Corinthians 13:13).

The book of Genesis tells of the first relationship between brothers. Six thousand years ago, after Cain killed his brother, Abel, God asked Cain where his brother was. Cain responded, "Am I my brother's keeper?" (Genesis 4:9b). As a result of his actions, Cain suffered the wrath of God. This story reminds us that we are accountable to one another. Brothers have a unique bond, although they rarely admit it. They are connected by a bloodline, experience, and permanence. You can choose your friends but not your brother.

David's younger brother, Stephen, had asked anxiously for daily updates and wondered how soon he could visit his brother in the hospital. The first two weeks were extremely hard on everyone, and I made the decision to shield Stephen from the brutal realities of David's condition. Although this decision was controversial, I wanted Stephen to miss all the graphic details we had to endure.

My wife, Renee, spoke to her nineteen-year-old son, Kyle, about David's condition. She tried to describe how David's skin had fallen off, but he asked her to stop because he felt nauseous and thought he was going to be ill. Kyle's response was further evidence that we were walking a tightrope as we dispersed critical information to the other boys. Renee began communication with her sons in a different manner due to this initial conversation. It was clear to us that the horror of David's condition went beyond what our children could accept at that stage.

I called Stephen every day with updates. He knew David's condition was extremely serious because I stayed at area hotels, keeping vigil at his bedside. Stephen had one eye on his schoolwork and the other eye on his brother's developments. I knew there was nothing he could have done for David except cry. But a part of him wanted to know the more realistic details instead of the optimistic viewpoint. I also noticed he was not yet ready to ask any probing questions. This indicated to me that, for the time being, Stephen didn't need any more information than we were giving him. I put off a reunion until David could participate as well.

On March 12, David was on the road to recovery and able to have visitors. Until that point, his visitors had been severely limited in order to minimize his risk of infection. Now he was free from his ventilator and eager to see his brother. I was grateful that my gamble to keep Stephen away didn't backfire. I would have regretted the decision had Stephen missed the opportunity to see David one last time.

David had progressed to the point that he was no longer in danger of dying. We had witnessed great improvements in his condition, but Stephen did not have the benefit of the contrasting before and after view. After picking up Stephen from home early one evening, I used the ninety-minute trip to prepare him with a more realistic view of David's condition. This face-to-face visit required a little finesse on my part to lower Stephen's expectations of the meeting. In the hospital parking garage, I took my last shot at providing a few more details of the horrific trauma David had endured over the past several weeks.

Stephen and I entered the hospital and made our way toward David's room. With each step, Stephen appeared to be collecting his thoughts. We walked through the ICU doors and passed the nurse's station to arrive at David's room. The lights inside his room were dim, and the atmosphere quiet. Stephen followed me into the room as if he were my shadow.

Stephen is six feet, one inch tall with a muscular, slim build, curly blond hair, and deep blue eyes. When he walked into the room, his eyes grew large as he looked at his tired brother. He proceeded to the bedside and stared at David for a few moments. From his perspective, David looked broken and weak.

Stephen noticed how thin and almost transparent his skin appeared. He held David's hand and commented on how soft it felt. His demeanor at David's bedside changed from curiosity and concern to compassion. David lay in his bed with his eyes closed, still exhausted from his ordeal. David tried to squeeze Stephen's hand for reassurance. However, his strength failed.

It was a tender moment for Stephen as he saw how the ravages of SJS TEN had affected his older brother. Stephen's presence was powerful as he connected with David. It was as if he were trying to transfer some of his strength to his brother. Stephen confided in me how proud he was of David and the courage it must have taken to fight through his pain the way he did. That night, he gained a new appreciation for the struggles his brother had been going through. I was proud of Stephen as he handled his brother with empathy and compassion. It was a beautiful moment I will never forget.

Together, these brothers have weathered many of life's storms. They each lost a beloved brother. God gave Stephen a second chance to appreciate his brother David in a profound way. The bond they share is a blessing beyond belief and makes this father proud. I could not have asked for better sons, and I am grateful for their hearts of compassion and love toward one another.

In the final analysis, Stephen and David embody all that is good and noble as they help one another along life's journey. Six thousand years ago, a brother asked, "Am I my brother's keeper?" The answer from Stephen and David is a resounding, "Yes, I am."

~ 19 ~

Finding Strength

*But those who hope in the Lord will renew their strength.
They will soar on wings like eagles; they will run and not
grow weary, they will walk and not be faint* (Isaiah
40:31).

Three weeks after his arrival by helicopter to U of M
Hospital in Ann Arbor, David was transferred to Crittenton
Hospital sixty miles away, in Rochester. This hospital was
much closer to our home and served as a next-step hospital as
they concentrated on his physical therapy. I was ecstatic, as he
was no longer considered critical. His illness had taken a
tremendous toll on his strength. He was not able to walk on
his own, nor did he have the strength to sit up by himself as
he began the next phase of his recovery.

Since he loved the arboretum at U of M so much, we
tried to find a similar type of environment for him at
Crittenton. The main lobby area provided the perfect place
for him to find relaxation outside his room. This large foyer
was the setting for his first reflections of his ordeal.

David sat in a wheelchair with his eyes still bandaged
when he first told us he had almost died. He viewed his hospital stay, along with every complication from his illness, as a
battle. He went on to explain he was pretty strong to have

beaten SJS TEN, and if he could defeat a calamity like that, he could also beat autism. He was still weak and his conversation limited; however, it was amazing to hear him put a positive spin on his experience. This affirmation was definitely out of character. In the past, I struggled without success to get him to see the bright side of even the smallest situation. Our family consistently tried to encourage him, but it was as if he couldn't hear us. I was surprised when he saw something positive in his ordeal. He'd gone through so much, it had been the most tragic event in his life, and he'd emerged with a positive attitude. As the days went on, it was astounding that he now viewed himself through the eyes of strength instead of weakness.

David was anxious to get back on his feet again. As time progressed, he began the process of standing with the aid of special shoes. They were lightweight and had a Velcro strap across the top so they could easily be fitted to his foot. The soles were made of foam-like material, which provided maximum cushion for the bottom of his feet by absorbing the weight of his body.

David's feet were extremely soft and fragile from the thin new layer of skin. He no longer had calluses on his feet because the skin layers had all peeled away. The new growth reminded me of baby skin. It was soft, smooth, and tender. Even with special shoes, he experienced a great deal of pain as he tried to stand on the thin new soles of his feet. Although he weighed less than 140 pounds, the weight of his body still created a great strain when he attempted to stand.

The membranes sewn on each of David's eyes at U of M were still intact. When he tried to open his eyes, it felt as if he had large foreign objects in them. Which he did. This in turn served as an immediate reminder to keep his eyes closed. The membranes left him temporarily blind. He was not able to use sight as a reference for balance, which in turn made his walking therapy more challenging. David felt a great deal of pain as he tried to stand and walk. The thin new skin on the bottoms of his feet left him with no calluses to cushion his weight. It is amazing to think how we take the smallest things for granted in our life. Have you ever thought of the calluses on your feet as a blessing? This was definitely a new concept for me.

Slowly, David pushed through the pain as he fought to achieve his goal of walking. In time, he grew stronger and stronger and at last, he could walk in the hospital corridors without his walker. He dreamed of one day running again down the streets and through the parks at home. Each day produced another hurdle to scale as he rose to the occasion and fought a great fight with SJS TEN.

On April 1, David was released from Crittenton to continue his recovery at home. He had a few restrictions, which he followed meticulously. He could walk without assistance; however, he lacked the strength to run. He was looking forward to returning to the sport he loved. The scar tissue had permanently damaged the tear duct in his left eye, so it did not function at all. Since his eyes couldn't produce sufficient hydration, he had to use artificial tears every ten to fifteen minutes of his waking hours.

David also had to apply moisturizing lotion several times a day, and his skin was too sensitive to expose to direct sunlight. He couldn't go swimming in a pool or take a hot bath. These obstacles seemed miniscule, compared to what he had been through over the last several weeks. He was finally home!

As time went on, he passed new milestones on his way to full recovery. It was truly a time of thanksgiving and celebration. We knew David would not be strong enough for a party on his twenty-first birthday, so we held the celebration in mid-May. Most young adults celebrate a twenty-first birthday as a rite of passage to adulthood, and adult beverages are often involved. This was not the case for David. He'd already completed his rite of passage—in the councils of heaven. We invited the family and friends who had traveled with us on David's journey by giving generously of their time, support, and prayers. His party was a powerful moment of reflection for everyone in attendance. A deep sense of rejoicing and awe filled the room as he fought to blow out his candles.

~ 20 ~

The Lamb from Heaven

No longer will there be any curse. The throne of God and of the Lamb will be in the city, and his servants will serve him (Revelation 22:3).

Several months after David was released from the hospital, I received a strange phone call from my wife, Renee. I was working second shift at General Motors at the time, and she was home making dinner for the family. David often came into the kitchen at this time to check out the menu. Her memory flashed back to his time in the hospital and how his body lay on an air mattress pumped with cold air. He'd shivered uncontrollably from a high fever. By nature, David was thin and hated being cold. She hoped he didn't have memories of this horrible event. She asked, "David do you remember being cold in the hospital?"

Much to her shock, he answered, "No, the lamb kept me warm."

"What lamb was that?"

"The lamb God placed on my lap to heal me."

Renee said she turned off the stove and had a conversation with David about his memory of his time in the ICU. She then called me at work and said, "You have got to hear about the conversation I just had with David."

The next day, I asked David about the memories he'd shared with Renee. As he told me the story, it was clear he was offering the exact account as before. He talked about dreams and visions as well as other experiences he had while in ICU. It was as if he could still see them in his mind's eye. Renee and I were stunned.

I wondered why months had gone by without any indication that something unique had happened to him during his hospital ordeal. However, when I thought about David's personality, it made perfect sense. His autism inhibited his speech, and he rarely volunteered information or initiated conversations. Such interaction contained risk for him. Sharing this experience would have been completely out of character for him.

He had not shared his experience because we simply had not asked him about his time in the hospital. In the early days of his recovery, we moved forward with his rehabilitation, trying desperately to distance ourselves from the pain and agony of the hospital experience. We did not want to focus on the past. We were hopeful for the future.

I did not know what to think when David first told us of his near-death experience. I had been exposed to this area of spirituality during my seminary years. However, I had never contemplated the possibility of this type of occurrence hitting so close to home. As I thought about the wonder of it all, I recalled all the unusual events and mini-miracles that had taken place in the hospital and how he'd miraculously survived. I started seeing a pattern that pointed directly to God.

David had an amazing story about a lamb that was placed on his lap to keep him warm and for his healing. The imagery from his experience was finding expression in his words. When I think about a lamb in Scripture, I immediately think of Jesus, who is the Lamb of God. This imagery has additional meaning when placed in context of the New Testament. I began thinking about Christ's additional titles and work on earth and how they related to our circumstances. I could find His influence in every extraordinary event. He consistently displayed in our hearts that He was in control. To us He is:

- The Good Shepherd, protecting us against danger
- The Light of the World, who gave us light when darkness loomed
- The Prince of Peace in the hours of uncertainty
- The Word of life, giving us strength to continue the walk
- God with us, helping us to feel His presence when we could no longer stand
- Author and finisher of our faith, giving hope and purpose in trials
- Deliverer from crushing defeat and profound sadness
- Mediator, revealing the blessings of heaven
- Rock, providing safety in trials
- Savior, the saving power of God

Two thousand years ago, on the banks of the Jordan River, John the Baptist proclaimed that Jesus of Nazareth was the Lamb of God, who takes away the sins of the world. He traveled the regions of Galilee, healing the sick of every affliction. The blind could see, the lame could walk, sickness was cured, demons were cast out, and the dead were raised to life. In many ways, we were recipients of all these blessings as the Lamb took on a new meaning in our lives.

The Bible often refers to Jesus as the earthly Lamb of God. David's testimony affirms that God is the ultimate healer. The symbolism of the lamb placed on his lap mirrors the biblical references to Jesus being the Lamb sent to redeem us from our sin-sickened state. In the book of Revelation, Jesus is also considered the heavenly Lamb. "'Then I looked and heard the voice of many angels, numbering thousands upon thousands, and ten thousand times ten thousand. They encircled the throne and the living creatures and the elders. In a loud voice they were saying:

Worthy is the Lamb, who was slain, to receive power and wealth and wisdom and strength and honor and glory and praise! (Revelation 5:11-12).

In Revelation 21:23, we read,

The city does not need the sun or the moon to shine on it, for the glory of God gives it light, and the Lamb is its lamp.

Jesus said in John 8:12,

I am the light of the world. Whoever follows me will never walk in darkness, but will have the light of life.

God has placed eternity in our hearts. We desperately need to use this time on earth to prepare for our home in heaven.

~ 21 ~

Intentional Miracles

You are the God who performs miracles; you display your power among the peoples (Psalm 77:14).

A miracle is an act of God that appears to be contrary to the laws of nature. It is an extraordinary event in the physical world that surpasses all known human or scientific explanation. When miracles occur in our world, God is often cited as the source because of the unknown yet supernatural nuance of the event. Therefore, we can view every blessing from God as a miracle.

The greatest miracle recorded in the Bible occurs in Genesis 1:1: "In the beginning God created the heavens and the earth." The Bible starts off with this incredible miracle. Throughout its pages, the Scriptures tell of a multitude of miracles that have already occurred, while others are reserved for the future.

By definition, miracles are rare and are usually events without a natural explanation. While some miracles are not repeatable, others can occur every day. We use the phrases, "The miracle of birth" and "the miracle of life." Each has its own unique parameters that are truly miraculous.

Miracles are often associated with mathematical probability and therefore can be discarded by the nature of random chance. For example, the probability of someone guessing all six numbers of a winning lottery ticket might be expressed as one in several billion. To some people, choosing the numbers correctly once in a lifetime would be a huge stroke of luck; after all, someone is bound to win. Therefore, accidently choosing the correct numbers would not be considered a miracle.

However, if someone played different numbers in twenty consecutive weeks and won each week, they would probably be arrested for fraud. No miracle here, either, and no luck. Miracles cannot be accounted for by luck or accidents. Miracles are intentional acts of God, designed for His purposes. Miracles impact the fabric and faith of one's life in unexplainable ways.

In our culture, we tend to think of miracles as robust, significant, and magical. The movie and entertainment industries portray miracles as magical feats that defy natural explanation. This definition, however, does not need to be the case as we look at miracles from a personal standpoint. Miracles could simply be God doing extraordinary works in our life, giving us opportunities that would not occur without Him.

Have you ever considered what makes a heart beat one minute and stop beating the next? The miracle of life, which we take for granted, will one day end. Natural death begins when the temporal miracle of life ends. Death is a process that ends life and functions as a bridge to a new existence found in eternity.

My definition of a miracle would include the simplicity of God intervening on our behalf. These mini-miracles occur when God causes circumstances to unfold in a way that changes the natural or expected outcome of the intended events.

Mini-miracles are less extravagant than the creation of the universe, or parting the Red Sea, or feeding the five thousand with five loaves of bread and two small fish. They are everyday, intentional acts of God that are directly related to answered prayer.

Below is a partial list of mini-miracles that occurred in and around the circumstances of David's illness. Some events may appear circumstantial, but my faith gives glory to God for every single one of them. Let's look at some of these situations, which are unusual to say the least.

David is 5'10" with a slim build and a weight that fluctuates between 125 and 140 pounds. He naturally prefers healthy foods and beverages. He never liked sodas of any type, nor did he drink any other sugar-based products. For six months leading up to his illness, his food preferences changed, and his weight jumped to 190 pounds. This weight gain was totally out of the ordinary for him. He did not binge eat, nor did he eat all the time. This new weight miraculously came in handy, as he appeared to need the extra pounds during his hospital stay. Six weeks after his hospital ordeal began, he had lost the extra fifty pounds as his weight returned to his normal 135 pounds, just as it once had. Seven years later, his weight is still 135 pounds.

The absolute necessity of correctly inserting a central line into David's neck was the first critical hurdle at U of M. The success of this surgery brought his body the lifesaving fluids and medication necessary to begin the process of healing. It was one of many mini-miracles that took place in the hospital.

In the early days of David's hospital stay, he was in total liver failure. It appeared his best chance for survival would include a liver transplant, but he was too ill to survive the operation. After a short period of time, his liver function returned to a non-critical state.

David's heart was in tachycardia, which means it was beating abnormally high at 140-160 beats per minute. Because of other complications, this rate could not be decreased by medication and stayed elevated for weeks. The doctors repeatedly mentioned that his passion for running kept his heart strong enough to sustain the stress the illness inflicted. David's lifestyle, which he chose years ago, helped to keep him alive.

David's fever averaged 103-104 degrees for ten days. We wondered how long his body could sustain such a high temperature before his brain or possibly other organs would be damaged. We didn't know if he would recognize us or would suffer cognitive impairment when he regained consciousness. He did not experience any additional problems as a result of his fever.

David's rapid regeneration of one hundred percent of his skin with no infection stunned the nurses as they unwrapped his bandaged body for the last time. This rapid regrowth of skin reduced the swelling in his airway, which allowed the doctors to remove the ventilator. He had been on a ventilator for fourteen days and was in danger of becoming dependent on it for survival. Removing the ventilator had become a priority. When it was out, I released a sigh of relief as he began breathing independently. He has only a vague recollection of touching his lips and being surprised the ventilator tube was no longer in his mouth.

David's near-death experience can also be considered a mini-miracle, because God not only provided physical healing for his body but also provided emotional healing for his life. His once-defeated and depressed attitude toward autism has been replaced with strength. His new mantra is, "If I can beat SJS, I can beat autism." For the first time in his life, he has self-confidence. His ability to interact with people has greatly improved.

As a grocery bagger at Kroger, one of David's duties was to tell the customers to "have a nice day" as they departed the checkout with their groceries. Prior to his illness, this simple requirement was nearly impossible for him. Each missed opportunity reinforced his self-image of being stupid and ugly. He surmised that he could not talk to people because he was stupid, and they did not want to talk to him because he was ugly. Our entire family was horrified when he explained his logic to us. We desperately tried to change the way he viewed himself. We spent hours in an effort to stop the constant flow of self-destructive ideas.

David is now capable of interacting with customers and has developed his own unique style as he tells his customers to have a good day. His ugly self-image has been replaced with the knowledge that he is a beautiful child of God. His transformation in this area alone is truly a miracle for him, as no amount of earthly encouragement could accomplish what his near-death experience achieved.

David has also been freed from one of the greatest fears we all face: the fear of death. He no longer fears his mortality or death because he has been given a preview of the wonderful future that awaits him in a beautiful garden full of light and love. He has already experienced moments without autism, and he wants people with special needs to understand that the grace and glory of God will also be part of their experience as they are freed from their current disability. God has shown him that there is no reason to fear death and that autism and other disabilities are only temporary.

It is truly impossible for me to understand the depth and numerous ways God intervened on David's behalf. God is a God of abundant miracles. I am grateful for every one, whether large or small. Miracles are real and God gave them all!

As Jesus walked this earth, He went about healing the sick, feeding the hungry, casting out demons, and raising the dead. His miracles did not end after He died on the cross, nor did they end at the resurrection. His miracles can be experienced in any generation. The last verse in the gospel of John may say it best:

Jesus did many other things as well. If every one of them were written down, I suppose that even the whole world would not have room for the books that would be written (John 21:25).

~ 22 ~

Redemption

I will give you a new heart and put a new spirit in you; I will remove from you your heart of stone and give you a heart of flesh (Ezekiel 36:26).

February 25 was a day that desperately needed to be redeemed. The horrific event of Michael's death, combined with the emotional pain and stress associated with profound loss, were deeply burned into my soul. His absence is heart-wrenching, and his memory inhabits my thoughts. His loss was devastating to me. My family and friends did their best to understand my feelings; however, my redemption needed to come from God.

When Michael died, friends and family went out of their way to avoid conversations that would elicit recollections of him. They walked on eggshells around me, not knowing if I was ready to reminisce about happier times. Unfortunately, no rules of etiquette dictate the appropriate time when a deceased child can be mentioned. I remember talking to a co-worker who told me she did her best not to remind me of the child I lost. I replied, "Do you think I could forget about Michael because he doesn't come up in a conversation?" Parents who have lost children think about them all the time.

Every year, I dreaded the entire month of February. My

only consolation was that February is the shortest month of the year. I was grateful for its lack of days. I went through a grieving ritual that included depression, anger, regret, and general numbness throughout the entire month. As the month progressed, I became distant from others and stopped caring about the routine of daily life. During the week leading up to the 25th, I just existed. I waited for the day to be over. I rehashed all the events in my mind. I could not escape my feelings of profound loss. My anxiety crippled any attempt to redirect my thoughts. I was a prisoner locked behind the doors of despair, hoping to forget many of the details of that day. But this type of memory has a tendency to leave a lasting imprint on the mind. Most days, I cannot remember what I had for dinner; however, I can remember what happened in great detail on that tragic day. Every year, I hoped somehow to find redemption for this day.

My sister June sends me encouraging, thoughtful greeting cards each year as she reflects on the memory of my son Michael. She includes loving and eloquent words of hope and comfort as she acknowledges the great loss I feel during this time. She articulates the feelings I cannot bear alone. I am grateful for her thoughtfulness as she shares my burden.

The redemption of February 25 arrived in a way I could never have imagined. February, 2009, started off with the same dread as previous years. However, in the week leading up to the 25th, David's illness did not give me time to think about the lingering pain brought by his brother Michael's death.

My time was spent ushering David to urgent care facilities and hospitals as his condition went from bad to worse to critical in what seemed like a blink of the eye. I simply did not have as much time or room in my thoughts to think about the child who'd died ten years earlier. I was focused on this child, hoping to prevent a reoccurrence of 1999. However, the horrible irony did not escape me as I struggled to resolve my diverging feelings. The urgency of David's condition kept my thoughts on the problems of the present day.

At first thought, I believed February 25 was a curse beyond belief. Each subsequent day reinforced my belief. As David fought for survival, my perception totally changed. As he recovered from this unbelievable nightmare, transformation took root in my heart. I started to see February 25 as a turning point. After his recovery, I shared with him how his determination to live had redeemed the 25th of February for me. I told him I would no longer remember February 25 with hopelessness, as I had in the past.

God has given me a precious second chance to view February 25th differently. I now remember the miracle of David's survival above the events of his brother Michael's death. I no longer intend to remember this day as the day I lost a son. Rather, I wish to remember this day as the day God intervened in a powerful way, and my second son survived. God had redeemed this day, as David's second chance became a reality. David is also grateful that his triumphant battle redeemed a tragic day in our family's history.

This second chance has given me the ability to enjoy the simple pleasures in life again as God gives them meaning. I have a deeper appreciation of all the subtle miracles that occur every day. As I watch David's faith grow, the tapestry of God is apparent within every aspect of his life. Additionally, the memory of the horrible events surrounding my first son's death have been overshadowed by God's provision and timing.

Sometimes the price for redemption is high. In my case, it took extraordinary measures to redeem one horrible day. Somehow, God perfectly orchestrated every event for me as February 25 marked the end of life for one son and the beginning of life for another.

~ 23 ~

Gratitude

Every good and perfect gift is from above, coming down from the Father of the heavenly lights, who does not change like shifting shadows (James 1:17).

David's near-death experience profoundly transformed his life. The once-timid young man suffering from depression and anxiety has changed into a man of conviction and strength. He personally felt God's love and his own identity as a child of God. In the garden of light, his self-image was completely renewed at a core level. Thousands of people prayed for his healing, but we never imagined the depths to which the prayers would be answered.

At times, in the hospital, I was blinded by sorrow and self-pity. Grief and despair consumed my thoughts, as I did not notice the mini-miracles or hidden blessings. My tears were like an ointment produced by my soul. Fortunately, my tears did not go unnoticed by God. He used the brutal circumstances to draw me to a greater understanding of His purpose. In this desert place, God combined these tears with the dew from heaven to produce still waters and provide an oasis of hope.

The mini-miracles provided proof of God's abiding grace. In times of despair, His provision is the only anchor that holds when all seems lost. God provided emotional and spiritual healing for both David and me. We give God the glory for the redemption brought about by His grace. As I stand on this foundation, gratitude is the outgrowth as my eyes were finally opened to the many blessings.

Several years ago, I stood on the Mount of Beatitudes in Israel. I could almost hear the ancient words of Jesus in the whispers of the wind as the Sermon on the Mount came to mind. Jesus said, "Blessed are those who mourn, for they will be comforted" (Matthew 5:4). How will those in mourning be comforted? By God using people to speak and help others as an extension of Himself. People who have gone through the fires of pain and anguish understand that emotions can be extremely raw in perilous times. The chosen few who have returned from the path of desolation can reside in His presence. Gratitude comes from a grateful heart that calls out to God to thank Him for all He is and all He has done.

Each of us can recall a time of great need. For some, it may have been a loved one going through suffering. For others, it was a failed relationship, a health issue, or mental instability. The good news is that God knows everything about you. Psalm 139:1-4 says, "You have searched me, Lord, and you know me. You know when I sit and when I rise; you perceive my thoughts from afar. You discern my going out and my lying down; you are familiar with all my ways. Before a word is on my tongue you, Lord, know it completely." God knows our pain.

This book is written as a testimony to God's abiding presence. I believe He is using the events of my life to help others who have been or are now in great distress. God comforted me in my darkest hours, just as He will you. These pages document a story of hope for the hopeless and help for the helpless. God will carry you in His everlasting arms of protection when the journey becomes desperately difficult. The events of February 25 have helped me to realize my previously undefined lifelong calling to serve God. He never wastes a tear. The waterfall of tears shed for the son I lost in death and the second son I almost lost have given me a profound understanding of death and sickness. I am currently working as a hospice chaplain, using my experiences to comfort those dealing with sickness and death.

I no longer believe the timing of David's illness on the tenth anniversary of Michael's death was a coincidence. His miraculous recovery would become one of the greatest lessons in gratitude I could ever imagine. Throughout the ordeal, my thoughts were with David, his health, and his recovery. The paralyzing influence generated by Michael's poor choice was preempted by the strength of David's fight to live. It is truly a strange dichotomy as a horrible memory of death was displaced by a powerful will to live. To say I am grateful would be a huge understatement. There are not words to express the depth of my gratitude to God.

David's near-death experience provided frosting on the cake of blessing. God walked with me through every detail of death's assault. I learned later that God also walked with David and angels comforted him as he experienced a glimpse of heaven few are destined to receive.

David's gratitude to God throughout his ordeal can be seen on many levels. He was blessed with a professional group of doctors, nurses, and hospital staff who used every means at their disposal to give him the best chances of surviving SJS and TEN. With his healthcare insurance, he had sufficient finances to cover the cost of the hospital stay. Everything about his life and exercise regimen worked together to fill in the critical gaps, which could not be controlled by medication. He had the incredible support of family, friends, and strangers who spent countless hours praying for him.

The near-death experience provided David with a new perspective on life. His insightful dreams and out-of-body experiences were proof that God has a specific, beautiful plan for him. He felt like a part of a much-larger mosaic, which God showed to him as his consciousness bridged two realities. In the beautiful garden of light, David had an understanding of what life felt like without autism. The confusion that plagues him on a daily basis was completely gone. True peace, joy, and love emanated from his heavenly encounter.

I believe the greatest lesson of my life occurred when David was finally healed. The lesson learned was gratitude. God used a time of incredible pain to bring about joy that surpasses understanding. He revealed Himself to us over and over again in the difficult hours of crisis. He freed my thoughts from darkness and grief, replacing them with thanksgiving and gratitude. Instead of focusing on the despair I once felt in February, I now redirect my thoughts to a greater good as God intervened in my life.

I have been given a purpose and a testimony to share with others traveling down similar roads, helping them find hope when disaster strikes. Just when you think your situation is hopeless, God can change everything.

I am confident that God worked miracles on a daily basis during David's ordeal. I am exceedingly grateful He allowed us to see His presence in the situation. The common dominator among people who have had a near-death experience is a profound gratitude for the encounter. Religious or not, people from all walks of life are compelled to thank God as they tell their stories of unique visions as great mysteries unfolded in their lives.

Jesus talked about the importance of thanking and acknowledging the gift of God through gratitude. The story is found in Luke 17:11-19 (NIV): "Now on his way to Jerusalem, Jesus traveled along the border between Samaria and Galilee. As he was going into a village, ten men who had leprosy met him. They stood at a distance and called out in a loud voice, 'Jesus, Master, have pity on us!' When he saw them, he said, 'Go, show yourselves to the priests.' And as they went, they were cleansed. One of them, when he saw he was healed, came back, praising God in a loud voice. He threw himself at Jesus' feet and thanked him—and he was a Samaritan. Jesus asked, 'Were not all ten cleansed? Where are the other nine? Has no one returned to give praise to God except this foreigner?' Then he said to him, 'Rise and go; your faith has made you well.'"

This story from Luke is designed to make a point. Recipients of God's grace and blessing are called upon to express thankfulness and gratitude to Him in response to His blessings. The account begins with ten men having a need for which there is no earthly cure. All ten are healed on their way to the priests. From these ten men, we see two types of responses: he who returns to express gratitude to Jesus, and he who does not return to thank Him.

This chapter is dedicated to the one who returned to thank Jesus for his healing. This Samaritan clearly understood it was Jesus who healed him as he journeyed to the priests. In the gospel account, the ten men went their way without Jesus touching them. He was not physically present with them as they traveled and were healed. It is clear these men were healed on the way to the priests.

Where were the other nine? Perhaps they believed they were healed as a result of walking in a hot desert. Or that the disease had naturally run its course without miraculous intervention. After all, Jesus never followed them, nor did He touch them. Jesus healed them from afar.

Years ago, our nation felt compelled to give public thanks and express gratitude to God for His blessings. President Abraham Lincoln created a resolution establishing a national day of prayer. He delivered his resolution to the United States Senate, and on March 30, 1863, it was signed into law. Oddly enough, the timing of this document was in the midst of one of the bloodiest events in our history. The Civil War had been raging for more than a year, and both armies had sustained heavy losses.

The following is an excerpt of this proclamation establishing a day of prayer:

> We have been the recipients of the choicest bounties of Heaven. We have been preserved, these many years, in peace and prosperity. We have grown in numbers, wealth and power, as no other nation has ever grown. But we have forgotten God. We have forgotten the gracious hand that preserved us in peace, and multiplied and enriched and strengthened us; and we have vainly imagined, in the deceitfulness of our hearts, that all these blessings were produced by some superior wisdom and virtue of our own. Intoxicated with

unbroken success, we have become too self-sufficient to feel the necessity of redeeming and preserving grace, too proud to pray to the God that made us!

This proclamation is a great example of gratitude and prayer in the midst of adversity. Just as Abraham Lincoln understood the importance of relying on God, we too should rely on God during our times of trials and testing. I am thankful to live in a nation with such deep spiritual roots.

Finally, I am grateful to the churches and prayer warriors who prayed daily for my family and for David's recovery. We were blessed to have family members and friends who drove long distances to join us in the hospital lobby to show their love and support. On the home front, colleagues from my wife's work as well as church members brought cooked meals and snacks to our home to help meet the needs of our other sons, as we spent most of our time at the hospital. I have much to be grateful for, but most of all for the Lord's abundant love, which was evident in the circumstances and people He used to aid and comfort us during our time of need.

~ 24 ~

A New Beginning

He who was seated on the throne said, "I am making everything new!" Then he said, "Write this down, for these words are trustworthy and true." He said to me: "It is done. I am the Alpha and the Omega, the Beginning and the End. To the thirsty I will give water without cost from the spring of the water of life (Revelation 21:5-6).

I am thankful my son David did not cross the barrier of death. At some point, he was aware he would return to his body, because he instinctively knew his work here on earth was not finished. At times, I feel his near-death experience has been much like a beautiful anointing from God as his second chance from heaven demonstrates a new purpose. His experience has turned out to be a profound blessing in his life. He realizes the strength God has given him to begin anew.

David's continued transformation has been amazing to watch over these past few years. God gave him a remarkable encounter in the heavenly realm, and it has profoundly changed his self-image. For years, he was defined by the limits of autism. This negative emotional aspect affected every area of his life. He can now see when he makes progress. He feels he has been given the strength to face each day. At work, David's social skills are being exercised as he now has the confidence to train new grocery baggers. He has made a few friends his own age and has become friends with two families. Additionally, he successfully completed two years of community college. He also attained a certificate in bookkeeping and desires to work in the accounting field. Each day, his autism appears to loosen its grip as he thrives in his current workplace and strives for a new career. He is an amazing young man, and I am proud of him and his accomplishments.

For the first time in his life, David is able to appreciate his surroundings and recognize the positive aspects of the world around him. The eternal garden of heaven is the lens he now looks through when problems arise. He has an acute awareness that his autism is, in fact, confined to this life and therefore temporary.

I believe one of the most significant events following David's experience is the transformation that has taken place in the way he views himself. His low self-esteem and poor self-image has been replaced with a view from heaven and the knowledge that he is part of God's wonderful creation. His perceived mirror of ugliness, which had tormented him day and night, was shattered in the garden of light. A new image emerged from heaven's perspective. He now sees himself as a beautiful child of God.

His near-death experience has given him renewed courage. He does not fear death or the afterlife because he knows he will be completely free from autism and surrounded by beauty and love. David is learning to conquer his fears and can now comfortably talk about issues that challenge him.

David's experience is yet another voice in a chorus of survivors who point to the way of salvation through Jesus Christ. He feels a kinship with others who struggle with the knowledge his experience has brought. This once-shy young man looks forward to having his story told and has no problem answering questions about his near-death experience.

Today, David also sees himself as a role model for others struggling with Asperger's syndrome. He has gone from being a person who was terrified to talk to anyone to a young man full of faith, who will tell his story to anyone who is interested. I am excited that God has given him a purpose and a story to tell to a skeptical world. David's story inspires people to reach out to God and trust Him when life's storms rage all around.

It is also important to consider the impact of David's story on other people. As we gave the progress reports to the churches and organizations that were praying for him, people were encouraged to see God working in his life. Many people felt a personal connection to the miracles and blessings David received. Prayer warriors were given hope by the story of this amazing young man. We were all in awe as the miracles unfolded before our eyes.

David's experience has provided a unique opportunity to share how God reveals Himself to people who are unconscious or close to death. To those who have loved ones in hospital beds, unconscious, fear not! God can speak to them in the background. David's testimony provides hope that God will not leave us, especially when we need Him most. There is a tremendous amount of comfort when we understand God is involved in every aspect of our lives, even in death's shadow.

David's experience allowed him to see himself as a beautiful child of God. Through his story, God has given him the ability to inspire others by sharing a view from the perspective of an eternal garden. If each of us could see ourselves from this perspective, imagine how our lives would change. It is my prayer that David's story touches your heart in a unique way. His glimpses of heaven transformed the way he views and lives life. He has been given an amazing opportunity to encourage others to see great hope as they rely upon God.

As this story draws to a close, I am thankful that God works all things for our good. He is present when the chaos of this life leads us down unknown pathways. When the road ahead is difficult, He guides us through the raging storms and delivers us from the torment of despair as He fashions the tapestry of our lives to lead us by still waters. He constantly covers us with blessings. He redeems us with the Lamb and gives us rest. His miracles are everywhere and He is closer than any brother. Finally, when death knocks, the whisper of eternity abides with our soul. He truly is a God who cares for us.

One day, there will be a homecoming, when God will reveal His glory to all mankind. All our tears and trials will be wiped away as God makes everything new. On that day, we will understand how the tapestry of our lives fits into the larger mosaic of mankind. If you are in the midst of struggles, rest assured that God is in control. He has a purpose and a plan for everyone.

How God will ultimately use David's encounter is still largely unknown. His amazing story has already encouraged countless people as he shares his experience in a garden of awesome wonder. God gave both of us a second chance when

He broke the emotional chains that had burdened us so long. It has truly been an honor for me to share David's extraordinary story. It is my prayer that you have found encouragement and strength to face any obstacles set before you in life. This wonderful account has given us a glimpse of peace, joy, and unconditional love in a kingdom that will stand forever.

From our entire family to yours:
The Lord bless you and keep you; the Lord make his face shine on you and be gracious to you; the Lord turn his face toward you and give you peace (Numbers 6:24-26).

Both riches and honor come from you, and you rule over all.
In your hand are power and might, and in your hand
it is to make great and to give strength to all

1 Chronicles 29:12-13

If you would like to know more
about Todd and David's story,
or see a list of upcoming appearances,
please visit
www.facebook.com/asecondchancefromheaven